W35

BASHABI FRASER is a transnationa[...] moves with ease between her two [...] Her publications include *Scottish Or[...] naissance: The Continuum of Ideas (*[...] *The Rabindranath Tagore and Patrick [...]* [...]*auer* (2017), *The Homing Bird* (2017), *Letters to my Mother and Other Mothers* (2015), *Rabindranath Tagore's Global Vision*, in a special guest-edited issue of *Literature Compass* (2015). Her awards include the 2015 Outstanding Woman of Scotland awarded by Saltire Society, Women Empowered: Arts and Culture Award in 2010 and the AIO Prize for Literary Services in Scotland in 2009. She has also had a special felicitation given by Public Relations Society of India as a Poet on International Women's Day in March 2017. She is a Professor of English and Creative Writing and co-founder and Director of the Scottish Centre of Tagore Studies (ScoTs) at Edinburgh Napier University. She is Chief Editor of the academic and creative peer-reviewed international e-journal, *Gitanjali & Beyond*.

ALAN RIACH was born in Airdrie in 1957. He studied English literature at Cambridge University from 1976 to 79. He completed his PhD in the Department of Scottish Literature at Glasgow University in 1986. His academic career has included positions as a post-doctoral research fellow, senior lecturer, Associate Professor and Pro-Dean in the Faculty of Arts, University of Waikato, Hamilton, New Zealand 1986–2000. He returned to Scotland in January 2001 and is currently the Professor of Scottish Literature at the University of Glasgow.

Thali Katori

An anthology of Scottish & South Asian poetry

Edited by

BASHABI FRASER and ALAN RIACH

Luath Press Limited

EDINBURGH

www.luath.co.uk

First published 2017

ISBN: 978-1912147-09-0

The author's right to be identified as author of this book
under the Copyright, Designs and Patents Act 1988 has been asserted.

The paper used in this book is recyclable. It is made
from low chlorine pulps produced in a low energy, low emission
manner from renewable forests.

Printed and bound by Bell & Bain Ltd, Glasgow
Typeset in 10.5 point Sabon

In memory of Jim Alison
who knew what good teaching is and how to make it happen

Contents

Foreword

Bleached Futures and Coloured Dreams

Thali Katori, published to commemorate the 70th anniversary of the Indian sub-continent's independence, immerses the reader in contrasting worlds of colour, climate and creed:

> *Edinburgh... a grey place*
> *for a Sikh who had looked on a golden temple*
> Christine de Luca

> *Happiness is tropical*
> Tessa Ransford

> *Krishna an Allah*
> *Twa wheels, the same barra*
> Sheena Blackhall

This anthology speaks to my heritage. My father was born in Delhi, five years before the trauma of partition and the upheaval of millions of people from their communities. In the early 1960s, he migrated to Scotland from Pakistan. A qualified stenographer, he met my mother in a jute factory in Dundee, where he found work when his qualification as a transcriber was not professionally recognised. Bashabi Fraser, co-editor of this anthology, has written about the bonds of the jute trade between Scotland and India, 'Made ready for / Bleached futures / And coloured dreams / On factory looms' ('Ganges to the Tay: Dundee Connection').

The civil servants who worked for the East India Company were known as 'writers', many of these were transcribers. It is estimated that by 1771 almost half of the East India Company's writers were Scots. As well as language, they brought with them the philosophies of the Scottish Enlightenment, which some historians claim to have had a positive influence on Indian nationalism. Language is political. Jeet Thayil observes in *The Bloodaxe Book of Contemporary Indian Poets* that, for many years, Indian writers in English were held accountable for nothing less than a failure of national conscience. This view was supported by Hugh McDiarmid: 'All dreams of "imperialism" must be exorcised, / Including linguistic imperialism, which sums up all the rest' (*In Memoriam James Joyce*).

The African-American reformer W.A. Dubois coined the term 'double-consciousness' where an individual can have two souls, two thoughts and two warring ideals. Growing up with dual Scots and Pakistani identity often felt like having to choose a winning side in a war of ideals. This isn't a universal condition. Jameela Muneer confronts this framing of identity through stereotyping: 'Caught between two cultures? / No Damn it. That's where *you* are / You've got an ethnic template / I won't get very far' ('I'm an Asian woman but…').

Ian Brown suggests that drawing comparisons between Scotland and India seems glib, 'Trying to appropriate what's powerful – akin, but distinct' ('A Tourist in Bishnupur'). Representations of the relationship between the two countries are hostage to many clichés associated with the British Raj. However, if one is searching for a synergy, as co-editor Alan Riach writes in this book's introduction, then it surely must be that of the experience of the Diaspora and the formation of attachments to the Motherland. Tariq Latif recognises this too, 'I recall the creamy keyre / my grandma used to make / early winter mornings' ('Walls of Mud').

Tessa Ransford, the founder of the Scottish Poetry Library, and whose work appears in this anthology, was born in India. Her father was Master of the Mint in Bombay and responsible for all the coinage for the British forces east of Suez. Among her first memories of Scotland were her bleak schooldays, where she was already writing poetry and discovering the work of Rabindranath Tagore which put her in touch with her 'Indian self'. This understanding and experience of the fluidity of identity led Ransford to champion and programme international writers and works in translation in the mission of the Scottish Poetry Library. In a similar vein, *Thali Katori* provides a platform for a multitude of voices, and it is to be commended that works by poets in Scots and Scottish Gaelic are included in this anthology.

Asif Khan
Director
Scottish Poetry Library
August 2017

Introduction

AT THE RED FORT in Delhi on 15 August 1947, Prime Minister Jawaharlal Nehru unveiled India's flag for the first time after British imperial rule had ended, on India's first Independence Day. On 15 August 2017, the seventieth birthday of that independence, imagine the Indian skies, alive with kites flying, strings held by folk on rooftops and in the fields, symbols of that independence. We thought it might be appropriate to compile an anthology of poetry from India and South Asia and from Scotland, to mark that occasion and to look into the complexity of identities and relationships that not only characterise these territories in themselves but also the relationships between them which have existed for over two centuries.

This complexity is described in a metaphor that gives us our title, taken from an essay on Salman Rushdie by the politician, diplomat and author Shashi Tharoor, in his collection, *Bookless in Baghdad: Reflections on Writing and Writers*: 'In leading a coalition government, the Hindu-inclined Bharatiya Janata Party has learned that any party ruling India has to reach out to other groups, other interests, other minorities. After all, there are too many diversities in our land for any one version of reality to be imposed on all of us.' Tharoor's conclusion is crucial: 'So the Indian identity celebrates diversity: if America is a melting pot, then to me India is a *thali*, a selection of sumptuous dishes in different bowls. Each tastes different, and does not necessarily mix with the next, but they belong together on the same plate, and they complement each other in making the meal a satisfying repast. Indians are used to multiple identities and multiple loyalties, all coming together in allegiance to a larger idea of India, an India that safeguards the common space available to each identity.'

'Katori' is a word signifying a small bowl, and a number of different foods might come in such bowls to go alongside the *thali*, one plate of an arrangement of separate, different and distinctive foods and flavours.

So *Thali Katori* brings together two words that celebrate difference, acknowledge the need of the sensitive appreciation of difference, the virtues of complementarity and the nourishment that poetry and the arts, as vitally as savoury and sweet dishes give us, to keep us alive, to refuse, in Hugh MacDiarmid's phrase, 'a life deprived of its salt.'

The universal metaphor of the nourishment provided for people by both food and the arts is less of a cliché and made more specific in the historical relations of Scotland and India, however. When Alan Riach visited India in 2016 to teach Scottish literature to students at Bankura University, West Bengal, in the first courses offered on that subject in India, the university Vice Chancellor, Professor Deb Narayan Bandyopadhyay provided some details about his own commitment to the teaching of Scottish literature. Most literature taught in India, he said, is traditionally canonical English literature, with extra and optional courses in American literature, 'New Literatures', Indian Writing in English and of course, literatures in Bengali and Gujarati and other Indian regional languages. Some scepticism from certain quarters had met his proposal to teach Scottish literature as a discrete subject. He had persevered with it for two reasons: first, there was no question about the quality of the material being as good as anything else; and also, the whole history of India and the country's relation to the British Empire was the context for studying the arts of his country. Now, increasingly, this also was understood to be the context for the study of Scottish literature. Such a course would be a study of literature, intrinsically, but it would also prompt questions about political history and future potential that need answers in the world we live in now. These answers only come through art. That value should be evident to anyone, he said.

So the history of an imperial power dominating a former colony and that colony then becoming an independent country might teach Scotland things of value; as much as a study of a country that has preserved its own distinctive cultural identities while, for just over three hundred years, being part of that British imperial project, might benefit students in the new India, in the 21st century.

The political history is rich, and troubling. In his *Autobiography* (1929), Gandhi wrote:

> I realised that the sole aim of journalism should be of service. The newspaper is a great power, but just as an unchained torrent of water submerges a whole countryside and devastates crops, even so an uncontrolled pen serves but to destroy. If the control is from without, it proves more poisonous than want of control. It can be profitable only when exercised from within.

That strikes deep in contemporary Scotland, where broadcasting is still a reserved matter for Westminster control and most of the newspapers are based south of the border. Then Gandhi issued a warning:

> What surprised me then, and what still continues to fill me with surprise, was the fact that a province that had furnished the largest number of soldiers to the British Government during the war, should have taken all these brutal excesses lying down... [Now] the reader [will be able] to see to what lengths the British Government is capable of going, and what inhumanities and barbarities it is capable of perpetrating in order to maintain its power.

But Gandhi also reminds us of the priority of peaceful resistance:

> It was clear that a new word must be coined by the Indians to designate their struggle... Maganial Gandhi coined the word 'Sadagraha' (Sat = truth, Agraha = firmness)... But in order to make it clearer I changed the word to 'Satyagraha' which has since become current in Gujarati as a designation for the struggle.

This implies not only 'passive resistance' or 'civil disobedience' but what is at the core of things that makes it all worthwhile: the primacy of 'Truth', of Swaraj, Home Rule, as a birthright and resistance to foreign domination through a non-violent strategy.

The struggle is experienced in this book not through politically explicit verse but through the distinctions of subtlety and suggestion, sensitivity and enquiry, the exercise of the imagination working through but also beyond the exigencies of any immediate political world. This is one of the virtues of the arts. We have deliberately included a diversity of voices and languages, cultural and religious backgrounds, poetic forms and forms of address, but we could hardly have done otherwise. The diversity is there. It's important to emphasise, however, that this is only a sampling of work that might be expanded into a much bigger book. Still, we hope that the selection of material will show a clear, if deeply patterned, trajectory.

We begin with Walter Scott and his friend John Leyden. The passage from Scott's novel *The Surgeon's Daughter* that opens our anthology was too good to leave out simply because it isn't a poem. What Scott is presenting in fiction here is an essential truth in all the arts. In Pablo Picasso's phrase, 'Art is a lie which makes you realize the truth.' Picasso also noted, 'Art is dangerous; yes, it can never be chaste, if it's chaste, it's not art.' The art in all the poems in *Thali Katori* adheres to these dicta.

We make our way through late Victorian imperial poetry, vividly compromised with divided loyalties, uncertain allegiances, or crazily wired to inexplicable enquiries and assertions in the work of L.A. Waddell; then on towards the overlapping tides of Empire withdrawing and Modernity coming in, with Violet Jacob, Rudyard Kipling and Hugh MacDiarmid, poems in Gaelic on Empire's meaning; and then, later, Tessa Ransford's moving prioritisation of the personal, bringing from her own experience a sense of what it is that makes life worthwhile. Coming into the late 20th century, we can see the move away from Empire's pretentious, dissembling assertions of certainty. 'Strong and stable' was a slogan used repeatedly by the Conservative Party leader in the 2017 UK general election. It's a phrase which comes directly from that world of imperialism and that's one of the reasons it feels stale and smells fousty. The distinction made by the modernist movement was to demonstrate forever the truth of multiplicity. There are 'eyes in all heads / to be looked out of' in Charles Olson's words. Or in John Berger's line, 'No story can now be told as if it were the only story.' And yet there are still people who insistently pretend that there is. That there is only one, single, imperial story, is a cliché being asserted by powerful people in various parts of the world. It goes with the phrase, 'There is no alternative.' But there is. Always. Against this, the poems in this book and all the arts are a living antidote, a material and immaterial help. Translations into Scots from Sarojini Naidu and Rabindranath Tagore are one way to show that antidote at work; lyrical poems about the personal experience of living in the context of a multicultural diversity of identities is another. Residents in Scotland, Scots, carrying in their mortal memories histories of a culture from beyond Scotland's borders, maybe coming from their own younger years, or maybe from their ancestors, demonstrate that; visitors to different parts of India, carrying in their minds their own histories of experience and nationality from Scotland, are others again. The trajectory unfolds in such complexity, but the story is not ended, of course.

In James Robertson's great novel, *And the Land Lay Still*, there's a memorable exchange between Saleem, the local shop-keeper, and his friend and regular customer, Don:

'Don, let me tell you what I think. My father was a government clerk when we lived in Delhi. He was an educated man. You could say we did not too badly under British rule. Please note my careful choice of word again. And then you could say that after independence everything went to rat shit for us. Yes, you could say that. We had to move and then we had to move again and it is only in the last few years, here in Wharryburn, that I have stopped moving. I don't want to go anywhere else. But what am I? I am a shopkeeper. What did my father, an educated man, become when he came to England? A bloody shopkeeper. I don't want to be a bloody shopkeeper any more than he did, but it is how he survived, it is how I survive. It is not the desired life, it is not the perfect life but it is a life. It could be worse. We could all have had our throats cut on a train. And yet, in all the troubles my father had, I never once heard him say, "Thank God for the British!" He didn't say, "Down with the British!" either but he knew that it was pointless being nostalgic about the past. I think you are too nostalgic about the past, Don. Does it offend you to hear me say this?'

Don laughed. 'Nothing you say could offend me, Saleem.'

'Don't bet on it. Let me tell you one more thing. I think you had better hurry up here in Scotland or you will be the last ones out of the British Empire and if that is the case, well...'

'Well what?'

'Well, you will look pretty bloody stupid.'

James Robertson is careful to make his characters enact the enquiries many people in real life get into trouble for articulating. This is what art can do. The poems in this book sometimes take up positions, sometimes refuse the option of such positioning and carefully prioritise the human universe above all temporal allegiances. Poems can do such things with ease. At the heart of them all, though, is that sense of the human diversity that Shashi Tharoor spoke of in the quotation with which we began. The population of Scotland is roughly 5.295 million; in 2015, the population of India was estimated at 1.311 *billion* (one thousand million). What could be comparable?

Perhaps that's the wrong question. Perhaps the question should be, what can we learn from each other?

Perhaps also, the question to consider is 'where is home' for those who have been scattered in colonial and postcolonial times, those who departed for other shores and those who arrived somewhere? Scots who left for India always felt they would come back 'home', yet some did not or could not as death or marriage or the decision to 'stay on' created a different or unintended narrative. In Kolkata (former Calcutta) there is the Scottish Cemetery where many Scots lie buried in a corner of India that will forever be Scotland. Their tombstones and the burial records tell the stories of those who never made it back to Scotland. For some of them, India was 'home'. And for those who did come back, they brought India back with them, in a Kashmiri shawl, an Indian servant, a wife, the taste for *chai*, the wish for the aroma of spices in their food, in words like *chhota hazri, piliwali, dulali*, the tantalising memory of the whiff of incense or the screech of kites flying against an uninterrupted Indian blue sky. The routes people took, sometimes voluntarily, sometimes coerced by circumstances – economic, political or social – the roots they then sent down, reluctantly, tentatively or deliberately, become significant here, as departures and arrivals mark the multiple journeys made by people moving between Scotland and India. In an interview with an Indian reporter, Benazir Bhutto, the onetime Prime Minister of Pakistan said, 'There is a fragment of India in every Pakistani,' which stresses the continuity of a shared culture and history that exists on the sub-continent in spite of Partition.

When Bashabi Fraser first came to Scotland in 1985, she came across several people who cornered her at dinners and receptions or hailed her on the street to ask her, 'Where are you from?' Her answer, 'From India' was the anticipated one, which brought on nostalgic memories of time spent in India, of a father who had served in the Indian army, a mother who was married in Calcutta, a cousin who went to school in Uti, an uncle who traded in Karachi or a grandfather who was born in Assam. Bashabi then went on to do several oral history sessions with Scots who had worked and lived in India and discovered that there was a fragment of India in every Scot, through friends, family members or ancestors who had some link with India preserved in personal journals, photographs, family film footage and artefacts brought back from India.

The South Asians

2017 celebrates 70 years of Indian Independence, which coincides with the formation of Pakistan and cannot be separated from the reality of Partition. In any consideration of modern South Asians,

the cataclysmic effects of the Indian Partition which saw the dis-
placement and dislocation of 14–18 million people after the stroke
of that historic midnight declaration, cannot be ignored. The peo-
ple who were affected by two mindless borders to create West and
East Pakistan, interrupted by 2000 miles of Indian territory, did
not desire or draw the shadow line(s). Many who found them-
selves on the 'wrong' side of the border, were forced to move. The
South Asian poets resident in Scotland today carry the memo-
ries of Partition and displacement through post-memory and the
stories they have heard from their parents and grandparents as
they face the reality of two, now three nations (Pakistan, India
and the transformation of East Pakistan into Bangladesh in 1971)
separated by borders, but knit inevitably by a cultural contigui-
ty and a shared history with Britain, and in this particular case,
with Scotland. Recalling Nehru's spontaneously delivered speech
at the midnight hour on 15 August 1947, we know that this was
how India redeem(ed)...(her)pledge, not wholly or in full measure.
Bashir Maan calls the South Asians in Scotland the 'New Scots',
and Herman Roderigues (in *Ragas & Reels*, 2012, with Bashabi
Fraser) refers to them as the 'broon Scots'. In a chapter on Scottish
South Asian poets, Bashabi writes, 'The New Scots belong to the
new diasporas that, unlike the old diasporic communities, are not
in a position where they cannot travel back to the land of their
forebears. Together with their parents, they retain cross-border
connections through travel and technological connectivity. They
have overstepped multiple boundaries... (they) cross and re-cross
borders of nations with affiliations, sympathies and contacts that
defy nation-state boundaries' ('The New Scots: Migration and Di-
aspora in Scottish South Asian Poetry' in Scott Lyall, Ed., *Com-
munity in Modern Scottish Literature*, 2016, pp. 231–232). So the
rupture that came with Partition is challenged and even surmount-
ed by today's South Asians in Scotland who identify with the con-
tinuity that exists 'here' in Scotland as they buy the spices from the
same shops and eat in 'Indian' restaurants which bring the flavours
from 'there' and they pick up their paisley patterns in shawls sold
in Scotland. As the title of one of Tariq Latif's poems says, the
South Asians in Scotland (like other immigrants and children of

immigrants) are 'Here to stay.'

This anthology recognises the fragments of India retained in Scots and South Asians, in the India Scots carried back with them after they or their forefathers returned from India and in the sub-continental links that are retained in Scottish South Asian poetry today. Tom Devine referred to Scotland as a restless nation at an Edinburgh International Book Festival event in 2011, and has said that Scotland's biggest export has been people. The transnationalism of Scots who have moved more than once, crossing regional and state boundaries with ease, from the islands to the mainland, the Highlands to the Lowlands, from Scotland to England before they departed on boats to the British Empire, is something they share with South Asians in Scotland, who have moved from India/Pakistan/Bangladesh across newly drawn borders, then journeyed to England or Canada, and finally came to rest on Scottish shores. During demonstrations in London after an attack on Asians in the 1970s, a banner the demonstrators carried said, 'We are here because you were there'. Such demonstrations have not happened in Scotland, but the historical statement does bring home the reality that the very shores that Scots landed on elsewhere and the people they encountered, are the lands from which the new fabric of the Scottish community, of a multicultural Scotland is woven today. *Thali Katori* brings home the flavours of this new Scotland-sub-continental relationship in an anthology that shows definitively a continuity that has existed between Scotland and India across two centuries from Walter Scott to Subhadeep Paul.

The dedicatee of this book, who is paid homage in one of Deb Narayan Bandyopadhyay's poems, knew this well. Jim Alison was a schools inspector. After his death in 2016, his family, with the support of the Association for Scottish Literary Studies and the Scottish Government, managed to get his extensive library of Scottish and international literature out to the University of Bankura in India, where courses in Scottish literature were being taught for the first time. It's a core foundation library of thousands of books, there for generations of students to come, and the best kind of international diplomacy you could imagine. Learning about other cultures, languages, religions, literatures, is the only way to move the world forward peacefully, with the eager appetite for learning any good teacher wants to encourage.

When Alan Riach visited in 2016, he wrote this:

And so to Bankura: through the crowded narrow dust-filled streets, people walking, cycling, driving all sorts of vehicles, cars, taxis, buses, vans, honking horns, or steadily walking carrying all sorts of things in bundles on their heads, past the kiosk-shops, dust-filled, grime-stained, grit-covered. The country all around is pastoral, cultivated, but every few miles there's a cement factory, an iron works, industrial workplaces. So most buildings look as though they've been burned and covered with ash, grey, grimy, brown. Some have collapsed, roofs propped up with thick bamboo poles. Intermittently there are bright new-looking buildings, sheer white and gold or turquoise, and among the dingy street-shops suddenly there's a shiny well-lit motor bike emporium or a computer shop. But the whole town is abundant with life. And there is no sense of smug, self-righteous resentment: scavenging, salvaging, finding things to help make life possible, is daily practice, everywhere you look. In fact, if anything is reminding me of the value of this visit, apart from the profession, teaching Scottish literature, it's that: here's a living world that says this is how we get on with things even in poverty and whatever circumstances, and it's not the Hollywood, *Jurassic Park* cliché, 'life will find a way': it's that life finds millions of ways, all sorts of things, strategies, methods, practices, all around.

That plurality was noted again by Shashi Tharoor in his essay 'God's Own Country' where he speaks of India as a nation and his native Kerala as a region, in *The Elephant, the Tiger and the Cell Phone* (2011):

I grew up in an India where my sense of nationhood lay in a simple insight: the singular thing about India was that you could only speak about it in the plural. The same is true of

Kerala. Everything exists in countless variants. There is no uniform standard, no fixed stereotype, no 'one way' of doing things. This pluralism emerges from the very nature of the place; for both Kerala and India as a whole, it is made inevitable by geography and reaffirmed by history.

Different specifics apply, of course, but in general, the same might be said of Scotland. It is an antidote to the priorities of single, central authority, single, uniform identity, supreme, imperial rule. The welcoming of difference and diversity, the common human purpose we might hopefully prioritise in our various arts, is what the poems collected here exemplify and celebrate.

Yet there is nothing bland or merely passive about this. Abundance and poverty, wisdom and ignorance, serenity and violence: extremes meet everywhere, but nowhere more memorably than in the conjunctions of India and Scotland, and the poems collected in this book represent and demonstrate the truths of such meeting, for sure. In an article in *Young India* (1 June 1921) Gandhi said:

I do not want my house to be walled in on all sides and my windows to be stuffed. I want the culture of all lands to be blown about my house as freely as possible. But I refuse to be blown off my feet by any.

This anthology shows how our poets have let the winds blow freely from elsewhere through their house, while they retain their own identity with dignity. As Nehru said in his midnight speech:

A moment comes, which comes but rarely in history, when we step out from the old to new, when an age ends... in this One World that can no longer be split into isolated fragments.

Thali Katori commemorates and celebrates this spirit of oneness and regeneration.

Bashabi Fraser and Alan Riach

Acknowledgements and Further Reading

We would like to thank all our contemporary contributors who have given permission for their work to be published in our anthology. We have drawn on numerous and various sources, online, personal and published. We would like to acknowledge the invaluable work of Mary Ellis Gibson, particularly her *Anglophone Poetry in Colonial India, 1780–1913: a critical anthology* (Athens, Ohio: Ohio University Press, 2011) and her book, *Indian Angles: English Verse in Colonial India from Jones to Tagore* (Athens, Ohio: Ohio University Press, 2011). At the other end of the chronological spectrum is the equally invaluable Kevin MacNeil and Alec Finlay, eds., *Wish I Was Here: a Scottish multicultural anthology* (Edinburgh: Morning Star Publications, Polygon, The Travelling Gallery and National Galleries of Scotland, 2000). Also crucially important in locating the Scottish Gaelic poetic tradition in an international context is Ronald Black, ed., *An Tuil: anthology of 20th century Scottish Gaelic verse* (Edinburgh: Polygon, 1999). Alison Lumsden and Douglas Gifford gave helpful advice regarding Scott's writing about India. The staff of the Scottish Poetry Library in Edinburgh were as always unfailingly gracious and helpful. Poems by Hugh MacDiarmid and Edwin Morgan are published by permission of Carcanet Press. John Purser was kind enough, and taken enough, to write a poem for this anthology which draws the great Scottish modernist composer Erik Chisholm into the picture. Purser's biography of the composer, *Erik Chisholm, Scottish Modernist (1904–1965): Chasing a Restless Muse* (Woodbridge: Boydell & Brewer, 2009) is essential reading for anyone studying modern Scotland and cultural internationalism. Chisholm's Piano Concerto No.2 'Hindustani' (1949) is available on Hyperion CDA67880 with Danny Driver, piano, the BBC Scottish Symphony

Orchestra and Rory Macdonald conducting. We all owe a debt of gratitude to Professor Deb Narayan Bandyopadhyay, Principal of the University of Bankura, whose commitment to the provision of Scottish literature in India is pioneering. His poem to the dedicatee of this book also acknowledges the work of one of modern Scotland's great champions of education and the democratic intellect, Jim Alison, whose legacy extends internationally in ways he might not have foreseen. For help through 2016–17 in removing his extensive library of Scottish and international books from Glasgow to Bankura, via Singapore and Kolkata, and thereby establishing a major foundational resource for the study of Scottish literature in India, we should thank the Association for Scottish Literary Studies and the Scottish Government. The arts are the only international diplomacy that really works.

Sometimes planning is required, and helps. Sometimes, though, the serendipity of the unpredicted also delivers good things. Thanks to all who have helped to make this book in that spirit.

We would like to thank the Andrew Tannahill Fund for Scottish Literature at the University of Glasgow. Every effort has been made to contact copyright holders; we will of course correct any inadvertent oversights in future editions.

B.F. and A.R.

Sir Walter Scott

From *The Surgeon's Daughter*

'I think you might do with your Muse of Fiction, as you call her, as many an honest man does with his own sons in flesh and blood.'

'And how is that, my dear sir?'

'Send her to India, to be sure. That is the true place for a Scot to thrive in; and if you carry your story fifty years back, as there is nothing to hinder you, you will find as much shooting and stabbing there as ever was in the wild Highlands. If you want rogues, as they are so much in fashion with you, you have that gallant caste of adventurers, who laid down their consciences at the Cape of Good Hope as they went out to India, and forgot to take them up again when they returned. Then, for great exploits, you have in the old history of India, before Europeans were numerous there, the most wonderful deeds, done by the least possible means, that perhaps the annals of the world can afford.'

'I know it,' said I, kindling at the ideas his speech inspired. 'I remember in the delightful pages of Orme, the interest which mingles in his narratives, from the very small number of English which are engaged. Each officer of a regiment becomes known to you by a name, nay, the non-commissioned officers and privates acquire an individual share of interest. They are distinguished among the natives like the Spaniards among the Mexicans. What do I say? They are like Homer's demigods among the warring mortals. Men, like Clive and Caillaud, influenced great events, like Jove himself. Inferior officers are like Mars or Neptune, and the sergeants and corporals might well pass for demigods. Then the various religions, costumes, habits, and manners of the people of Hindustan, – the patient Hindhu, the warlike Rajshpoor, the haughty Moslemah, the savage and vindictive Malay – Glorious and unbounded subjects! The only objection is, that I have never been there, and know nothing at all about them.'

'Nonsense, my good friend. You will tell us about them all the better that you know nothing of what you are saying; and come, we'll finish the bottle...'

John Leyden

Ode to an Indian Gold Coin

Slave of the dark and dirty mine!
What vanity has brought thee here?
How can I love to see thee shine
So bright, whom I have bought so dear? –
The tent-ropes flapping lone I hear
For twilight-converse, arm in arm;
The jackal's shriek bursts on mine ear,
When mirth and music wont to charm.

By Cherical's dark wandering streams,
Where cane-tufts shadow all the wild,
Sweet visions haunt my waking dreams
Of Teviot loved while still a child,
Of castled rocks stupendous piled
By Esk or Eden's classic wave,
Where loves of youth and friendships smiled,
Uncursed by thee, vile yellow slave!

Fade, day-dreams sweet, from memory fade! –
The perish'd bliss of youth's first prime,
That once so bright on fancy play'd,
Revives no more in after-time.
Far from my sacred natal clime,
I haste to an untimely grave;
The daring thoughts that soar'd sublime
Are sunk in ocean's southern wave.

Slave of the mine! Thy yellow light
Gleams baleful as the tomb-fire drear, –
A gentle vision comes by night
My lonely widow'd heart to cheer;

Her eyes are dim with many a tear,
That once were guiding stars to mine:
Her fond heart throbs with many a fear! –
I cannot bear to see thee shine.

For thee, for thee, vile yellow slave,
I left a heart that loved me true!
I cross'd the tedious ocean-wave,
To roam in climes unkind and new.
The cold wind of the stranger blew
Chill on my wither'd heart: – the grave
Dark and untimely met my view –
And all for thee, vile yellow slave!

Ha! comest though now so late to mock
A wanderer's banish'd heart forlorn,
Now that his frame the lightning shock
Of sun-rays tipt with death has borne?
From love, from friendship, country, torn,
To memory's fond regrets the prey,
Vile slave, thy yellow dross I scorn! –
Go mix thee with thy kindred clay!

George Anderson Vetch

On Visiting the Grave of Lieutenant Kirk, in Nepal

'Midst scenes as his own Grampians wild,
Here lies the Virtuous and the Brave –
On hills sublime his Cairn is pil'd
Where torrents dash – and pine-trees wave.

With Pilgrim-steps by sorrow led
O'er Mountains wild, remote, and drear,
I come the bursting tear to shed,
And kneel beside thy early bier.

I little thought of this thy doom,
When in farewell I press'd thy hand,
Our trysting place thy mountain tomb!
Amidst this far romantic land.

Where sweetly winds the past'ral Tay,
Thy native worth was early known,
Which still through Ind's subduing day,
With undiminish'd lustre shone.

And now thy years of exile o'er,
Thy breast beat high at Scotia's name:
Prepar'd to seek her happy shore,
A Son she might be proud to claim.

But Heav'n which still directs the best,
The long fond cherish'd wish denied –
Submissive to its high behest,
Serene the Christian Soldier died.

On a Canary Bird

That died suddenly after nearly concluding the voyage to India

Alas our little warbler's dead –
Its spark of Minstrel-fire is fled –
For ever hush'd the thrilling lay
That cheer'd us on our weary way!

Ah me, 'tis surely more than death
When dies the Minstrel's tuneful breath –
'Tis not these glazing eyes declare
That life no more shall brighten there:
But where's the power that bore along
So late the magic gift of song?
Can that high ton'd and heav'n-taught quaver
Be in a moment hush'd for ever?
In life – whence was its pealing tone,
In death – whence is its spirit gone!

How sweetly with the rising sun
Thy matin hymn'd the new born day: –
And must I ere the day be done
Pour with my tears thy requiem lay!
O had I known thy last farewell
Was breath'd in that delighting swell,
Mine ear had drank with grief the strain
It never was to hear again.
And shall I not lament for thee
Companion o'er the dark blue sea –
Like us an Exile from green bowers
And sharer of our prison-hours –
For thee – with whom I claim a part
In Minstrelsy's extatic art –
For thee – with whom we've circled o'er
The wide, wide world – for thee no more.

O far from nature's living green
Thy song recall'd the rural scene –
Sweet as the Lark o'er Scotia's Lea
Thy notes resounded o'er the Sea.

Haply thy now glad spirit roves
Delighted through thy native groves –
And from its cage and Ocean free
Wakes songs to woodland Liberty;
If so, I love such scenes too well
To wish thee back in prison-cell;
But we shall miss thy blithesome lay
On Ocean's long and dreary way –
And on sad India's blazing plains
Unblest by warbler's rural strains:
O till my native hills I see,
Sweet Minstrel, I shall mourn for Thee.

The Exile's Tribute

What Bard a votive lay may bring
In honour of the Chief of Song?
The loftiest lay would do him wrong,
Unless another Burns should sing.

A pilgrim at our Minstrel's shrine,
Where Nature wakes with morning's fire
The echo of his thrilling lyre,
To stand in grateful tears be mine.

How oft when sad, and far away,
The melting voice of Coila's Bard
In all the 'joy of grief' was heard
To triumph o'er the exile-day.

Condemn'd 'neath tropic skies to roam
Where scorching winds o'er deserts blew,
The mountain daisy bathed in dew,
Restored the hills and streams of home.

There, where no bird's sweet warblings rise,
To gladden India's dreary plain,
I heard in Burns the laverock's strain
Rejoicing in my native skies.

Wand'ring forsaken, and forlorn,
The Bard of Love's entrancing power,
Recalls the bliss of gloamin'-hour,
And vows beneath the trysting-thorn.

The friendships that beside the Tyne
Endears the scenes of joyous youth,
Rush'd back thro' tears in all their truth
To live again in 'Auld Lang Syne'.

When far from my own village spire,
And idols claimed each horrid rite,
O, with what sacred, pure delight,
I worship'd at the Cottar's fire!

And when to war the trumpet rung,
With what a high, exulting glow
The sons of Scotia met the foe
As men from Bruce and Wallace sprung!

Where'er a home-sick exile mourns
The vanish'd joys of early years,
The anguish of impassion'd tears
Finds utt'rance in the song of Burns.

Kings may expire, and states decay,
But long as lovely Nature reigns,
Her laureate-bard's attending strains
Will hold their everlasting sway.

James Ross Hutchinson

Moonlight Scene

On Ganges' stream the moon shines bright,
And swift the skiff glides on its breast;
The waves are rippling in its light,
And all is fair and still, at rest.

The stately palm, its banks along,
High rears its head amid the trees;
There's scarce a breath to wake the song,
Its leaves sing, nightly, to the breeze.

A hundred barks at anchor ride,
The neighbouring city's walls below;
The lordly domes upon its side,
Far o'er the wave their shadows throw.

There is a stillness in the hour,
There is a magic in the scene,
That o'er the spirit hath a power,
To wake the thought of what hath been.

Song

What ails this heart o' mine?
What ails this watery e'e?
What gars me aye turn cauld as death,
When I take leave o' thee?

What makes the hours o' day
Gae by sae light and free,
Till hours, like minutes, fast fell by,
Because they're spent wi' thee?

Why shuns sweet sleep these eyes?
The night seems long to me?
I see thee, hear thee, but by day;
At night I meet not thee.

Yet aft will sleepless fancy rife,
Like Seer's prophetic e'e,
With scenes which are, yet are not life,
In dreams return to thee.

David Lester Richardson

Sonnet – On Hearing Captain James Glencairn Burns Sing (in India) His Father's Songs

How dream-like is the sound of native song
Heard on a foreign shore! The wanderer's ear
Drinks wild enchantment, – swiftly fade the drear
And cold realities that round him throng,
While in the sweet delirium, deep and strong,
The past is present and the distant near!
Such sound is sacred ever, – doubly dear
When heard by patriot exiles parted long
From all that love hath hallowed. But a spell
Ev'n yet more holy breathes in every note
Now trembling on my heart. *A proud Son sings*
The lays of BURNS! Oh! what imaginings
Awake, as o'er a foreign region float
These filial echoes of the father's shell!

Calcutta, 7 August 1833

View of Calcutta

Here Passion's restless eye and spirit rude
May get no kindred images of power
To fear or wonder ministrant. – No tower,
Time-struck and tenantless, here seems to brood,
In the dread majesty of solitude,
O'er human pride departed – no rocks lower
O'er ravenous billows – no vast hollow wood
Rings with the lion's thunder – no dark bower
The crouching tiger haunts – no gloomy cave
Glitters with savage eyes! – But all the scene
Is calm and cheerful. At the mild command
Of Britain's sons, the skilful and the brave,
Fair Palace-structures decorate the land
And proud ships float on Hooghly's breast serene!

Sonnet – The Suttee

Her last fond wishes breathed, a farewell smile
Is lingering on the calm unclouded brow
Of yon deluded victim. Firmly now
She mounts, with dauntless mien, the funeral pile
Where lies her earthly lord. The Brahmin's guile
Hath wrought its will – fraternal hands bestow
The quick death-flame – the crackling embers glow –
And flakes of hideous smoke the skies defile!
The ruthless throng their ready aid supply,
And pour the kindling oil. The stunning sound
Of dissonant drums – the priest's exulting cry –
The failing martyr's pleading voice have drowned;
While fiercely-burning rafters fall around,
And shroud her frame from horror's straining eye!

L.A. Waddell
From: *The British Edda*

From 'Scene 1: Vision of Eden & Its Serpent Priestess
& Pre-Adamite Peopl'

The Three Fate Weirds in Eden
& their Sacred Tree

Thence came the maids (of Ymi)
With their manifold witchery;
Three o' them in the cell
That 'neath the Tholli-tree stands.
Urd weird is one named,
And another Verdandi,
Shearing on the Fate-sticks;
Skul the binder in the third.
They heard the Logos Word (of 'Fate')
They lived in a trance;
For those born of old
They were the weirds and soothsayers.
Standing far to the north
At the Nether Fell
Is the cellar of Gulli
Of this cindry race.
And yet another cellar
Stood at Okolni,
The beer-cellar of the Edenite
Brimi, the Burner, he's named.
Heidi and Horse-thief (Wodan)
Were of the Hrimni kin.
OEl (El Heide) begat Wolf Loki (Baldr)
By angry Bodo (Wodan):
That slippery one (she) begat
With Swad-the-ill-farer (Wodan)

45

That adder-thoughtful scarer (Loki)
With all his fearful lust.
[.....]
Edenites all of them
Come from Ymi (of Hell).

Atrocities of the Serpent Priestess

Hurt reigned in her home
And much houridom.
A club-age, an axe-age
With butchery cleaving.
A wind-age, a wolf-age,
Ere the old world riot was stopt:
Men tore other men untiring.
There, the Nether Ogress sucked
Mankind in misfortune;
The she-wolf Frigg slit the men!
Know ye then the Edda?
Know ye yet it all?

Full long she pauses,
The prudent balladist.

Violet Jacob
From: *Poems of India*

Night in the Plains

The plains lie in the furnace of the year
And sleep, repenting, hides from men his boon,
And flagging life strains fitfully to hear
The tardy footstep of the slow monsoon.
All day the stones, the dust upon the plain,
From never-changing skies the heat have drawn,
And darkness brings no solace in its train
– The breeze will rise an hour before the dawn.

There is no rest; from out the heavy skies
The burning planets hang; now near, now far,
Shrilly the women's voices fall and rise,
Crying to Kali in the hot bazaar.
There is no nightwatch but will end at last,
There is no vigil but will pass away,
The time wears on, the moon is setting fast
– The breeze will rise an hour before the day.

Life crouches low and fear is with the strong,
On every side the crawling time to mark,
There sound, like fevered pulses all night long,
The tom-toms, throbbing in the stifling dark;
A puff of odour from the jasmine-tree
Comes by the well across the parching lawn,
See where the hosts of heaven stand patiently,
– The breeze will rise an hour before the dawn.

The sick men toss, the breathless air is still;
Along the ward one slow, soft whisper falls,
Where Death's grim angel waits to have his will
Within the shadow of the whitewashed walls;
And women's steadfast eyes are fixed upon
The lurking shape whose hand they keep at bay,
Stand up, O souls of men, fight on, fight on!
– The breeze will rise an hour before the day.

Is that a shiver in the tamarind,
Or some awakening bird that stirs the leaves?
Turn, turn to sleep, there comes a breath of wind
And mainas talk by the verandah-eaves;
A little space to sleep and to forget
Before the tyrant sun begins his sway,
Ere in the heavens his brazen throne be set
– God give us strength to face the coming day.

The Resting-place

Brother, beside the jungle track, thy stone
Half raised, a nameless, carven slab, I see,
Half hidden by the tangle, secretly;
Where roots join twisted hands above thy head,
Where scarce a footfall passes save my own,
Nor white man's tread.

I have been wandering since noon was high,
And now, because the evening comes apace,
Thy tomb shall be my rest a little space;
From thy long-vanished hand this loan I take,
Across the years this hospitality
That thou dost make.

The jungle has grown over thee, O friend,
For, scarce a furlong from thy buried dust,
Once stood a city where the great and just
Built high the parapet and mosque and dome,
Where now the creeper flings its tasselled end
Around their home.

How many centuries have come and gone
Since first thou sawest, with awakened eyes,
The green-scarfed houris proffering Paradise;
Since thy young crescent moon, athwart this shade,
Son of the Prophet, has in silver shone
Where thou art laid!

Mayhap, thy spirit loved what mine loves best;
The tread of horses and the pride of life,
The jungle's magic and the joy of strife,
The long nights spent beneath the spangled sky –
O dead Mahommedan! Thy passing guest
By these accepts from thee this meed of rest
Salaam, O Bhai!

Evening in the Opium Fields

As pageants, marshalled by a masterhand,
So are the poppy-fields; in rose and red
And foam of white and livid purple spread,
Mile upon mile, they stretch on either hand;
Dark by the well the heavy mangoes stand,
Where labouring oxen pace with dusty tread
And dripping water-skins climb up to shed
Their gush upon the irrigated land.

So cool the labyrinthine channels run,
Flooding the grey stems with a maze of gold;
For, as he nears his end, the dying sun
Does all the plain within his arms enfold;
Beneath the mango-trees long shadows creep,
Like sleep's tread falling through the flowers of sleep.

'God is Great'

'Allah hu akhbar!
'Allah hu akhbar!
La ilaha illalah!'

Aslant upon the dusty way
The little mosque has thrown its shade,
A streak of blue at noontime laid,
To lengthen tardily with day;
And now the hour has come to pray,
Soldier and prince and clod –
'God is great, God is great,
There is no god but God!'

He stands upon the outer wall,
His hands upraised, his sunken eyes
Look westward to where Mecca lies;
Ho! Islam's men, it is the call
To evening prayer; he cries to all,
Soldier and prince and clod –
'God is great, God is great,
There is no god but God!'

Close to the wall below his feet
A pomegranate, against the white,
Flaunts, green and scarlet, in the light,
Now glaring day has lost its heat;
Ho! Islam's men in field and street,
Soldier and prince and clod –
'God is great, God is great,
There is no god but God!'

Dark figure, seeing inwardly
Through evening mist and evening balms
To Mecca, white among the palms,
Across the rolling leagues of sea,
At thy long cry they bend the knee,
Soldier and prince and clod –
'God is great, God is great,
There is no god but God!'

Spread at thy feet, around, beneath,
The world wears on amid its tears,
And few and evil are their years
Fighting their way from birth to death,
Soldier and prince and clod –
What shining city canst thou see,
Far off, beyond the flood of fate,
Where none are poor or desolate
That thou dost cry eternally?

There comes no answer, early, late,
But 'God is great, God is great,
There is no god but God!'
'Allah hu akhbar!
'Allah hu akhbar!
La ilaha illalah!'

Cherry-blossom at Dagshai

Far down below this range today
A waft of morning pureness fills
The blue ravines that stretch away
To lose themselves among the hills.

And, like a shrouded diadem,
Beyond the peaks set row on row,
Looms northern India's mystic gem,
The crown of Himalayan snow.

These lower heights which close us in
A more ethereal jewel wear,
There seems, where sheer descents begin,
A radiant mirage in the air,

For, with its veil of rose and foam
A-quiver like transparent wings,
To the stern ramparts of its home
The wild hill cherry-blossom clings.

Own sister to the clouds of dawn,
Each magic tree o'erhangs the brink,
Its slender stems like lattice drawn,
Dark, on a fairyland of pink.

Three days agone no sign was ours,
No voice to cry the coming hope
That autumn's wave would break in flowers
And roll in torrents down the slope;

But as, when darkness rends apart,
A shaft of glory pierces through,
Joy's hand has pierced the mountain's heart
And all the barren world is new.

The Distant Temple

Branch of the henna-tree,
Blown in a temple garden far away
In that unfading East across the sea,
O for one waft of perfume from your spray
To cheer the heart in me!

Flower of the champa white,
Sown by the evening wind where dusky feet
Have worn the temple pavement with their beat,
I would lie down and give my soul to-night
Could I but breathe your sweet!

Note of the temple gong
At sunset clanging through the dusty gold,
Since last I heard your nightly music told
It seems as though the months were ages long
And joy itself grown old.

Heart of the East, my heart,
Laden with your remembrance, may not rest;
The very winds that blow from east to west
From out that far horizon-line, impart
Your whisper, trebly blest.

Sound of the temple drum,
Like distant beating of the march of fate,
Through the long years your voice is never dumb,
Calling, at sundown, from the temple gate
To me, who cannot come.

Aonghas Moireasdan / Angus Morrison

Bho 'Smuaintean air Mòrachd Ìmpireachd Bhreatainn'

Cia lìonmhor feart as leat o d' theachd gu d' thriall,
A ghréin as oirdheirc siubhal bhon ear gu'n iar;
Cia lìonmhor subhailc fialaidh ann ad' ghnùis,
Cia lìonmhor beannachd dòrtadh air gach taobh!
Air Ìmpireachd Bhreatainn 'freastal oirr' a-ghnàth
An ear no 'n iar, an tuath no 'n deas gun tàmh,
Cha laigh an dùbhlachd oirre seo gu léir –
Do sholas deàlrach 'soills an àird nan speur
An àiteigin 's a' bhratach togt' ri crann
An-siud no 'n-seo is thusa gràsail ann;
Mi 'n dòchas nach tig ortsa caochladh rian,
Is thusa maireann, Breatann, mar an ciand'.

Có chuireadh smal air Breatann aoigheil, chòir?
Ar màthair thu rinn còmhnadh oirnne 's fòir,
Muim-altram thu gach dùthcha tha fon ghrian;
Do thabhairt suilbhir cha d'rinn bochd thu riamh,
Sgaoil thu do dhuilleag ghorm thar bhàrr gach fonn –
Do fhreumh, do stoc, do mheanglain làidir buan;
Mar s mòid do thabhartas ro mhòid do mhaoin,
Cha robh thu balbh ri feumalachd cloinn daoin';
An t-eilean beag a' boillsgeadh anns a' chuan
Mar sheud ro phrìseil sgapas foidhneal uaith',
Mar lòchran deàlrach tilgeil solas-iùil
Do mhuilleanan air seachran cuan an t-saoghail;
Do mhuirichinn sgaoileadh iad air raon is bheann
Mun iadh a' ghrian an sliochd gum faighear ann
Is aitreabh thogadh leo is bailtean mòr'
Le laghan ceart gun fhiaradh clì on chòir,

Le grìd is spìd air taille dìchill chruaidh;
Ge cruaidh an gleac, gu diongmhalt' ràinig buaidh,
Gun chìosnaich daoine borba 's coille 's fonn,
An colann slàn 's an inntinn làn de chonn –
Ged fhuair iad freumh is sìol an dùthaich ùir,
Air am màthair Breatainn cha do thionndaidh cùl.

From 'Thoughts on the Greatness of the British Empire'

How manifold your strength from your coming to your going,
O sun whose course from east to west is so magnificent;
How manifold the generous virtues in your countenance,
How manifold the blessings pouring on each side!
Upon the British Empire shining always
In east or west or north or south unceasing,
The dark will not descend on it entire –
Your brilliant light is shining in the skies
On some place where the flag is raised
Here or there where gracefully you are;
I hope no change of state befalls you ever,
And that you, O Britain, will be no less lasting.

Who would besmirch hospitable, kind Britain?
You are our mother who gave us help and succour,
Fostermother you are of every land on earth;
Your cheerful giving never made you poor,
Across the surface of each land you've spread your foliage green –
Your root, your trunk, your branches strong and lasting;
The more you give away the more your wealth increases,
You were not dumb to needs of human beings;
The little island shining in the sea
Like priceless jewel that sparkles far and wide,
Like shining lantern casting guiding light
On millions scattered across the oceans of the world;
Your offspring have been spread on hill and plain
Until where sun encompasses their progeny is found
And homesteads built by them and cities too
With proper laws unbending from the right,
With excellence and energy resulting from sound diligence;
Though hard the struggle, triumph was firmly reached,

They conquered savages and wood and land,
Their bodies healthy and their minds replete with sense –
Yet for all their roots and seed in pastures new,
On their mother Britain they've not turned their back.

Rudyard Kipling

Prefatory poem to *Departmental Ditties*

I have eaten your bread and salt,
I have drunk your water and wine,
The deaths ye died I have watched beside,
And the lives that ye led were mine.

Was there aught that I did not share
In vigil or toil or ease, –
One joy or woe that I did not know,
Dear hearts across the seas?

I have written the tale of our life
For a sheltered people's mirth,
In jesting guise – but ye are wise,
And ye know what the jest is worth.

Hugh MacDiarmid (C.M. Grieve)

From 'Lament for the Great Music'

It is world-wide, ageless. It is the Sufi *Nida and Saut*;
It is the Indian *Ragas*, and melodies of the old *slokas* and *ghazals*,
Deliberately cast in an animal function, whereas poetry and music,
Involving no bodily activity of the artist in their making,
Can exist in a purely psychological relation to society
And would be equally 'true' in a world of disembodied spirits;
And, as Plato knew, it is futile for artists
To discuss subtle distinctions, nuances of the scale,
And listen as though they sought to discover secrets,
While all of them in the practice of their art neglect
The theories of the mind and follow nothing but the law of their
own ears.
The supreme reality is visible to the mind alone.

From *In Memoriam James Joyce*

Let us arise,
We whose 'calf-country' is Siksha,
The science of proper pronunciation, and the grammar of Panini.
Beyond all grammars for originality of plan
And for analytical subtlety – Panini
Fabled to have seen rather than composed
This 'natural history of the Sanskrit tongue'
In Sütras which are perfect miracles of condensation,
The maximum abridgement being effected by the coining
Of an arbitrary symbolical language,
The key to which must be acquired
Before the rules themselves can be rendered intelligible.
– The closing Sütra shows the consummate brevity attained.
It reads merely 'a a', which is said to mean
'Let short a be held to have its organ of utterance
Contracted, now we have reached the end of the work
In which it was necessary to regard it as otherwise.'
– Grammar regarded as we should regard the natural sciences,
Something to be studied and elaborated for its own sake
– And so on to Kätäyana's Värtikas
Or 'supplementary rules and annotations'
And to Patanjali's Mahabhashya or 'great commentary'
And to the hundred and fifty grammarians and commentators
Who followed in the footsteps of that great triumvirate,
Each criticising or commenting on his predecessors –
Kaiyata, Vamanan, Bhattoji-dïkshita,
To Madhyama-kaumudï, the laghu-kaumudï of Varada-rä ja,
Vopadeva – we know them all
And every detail of their works [...]
– All dreams of 'imperialism' must be exorcised,
Including linguistic imperialism, which sums up all the rest.

From 'The Snares of Varuna'

The world is fast bound in the snares of Varuna
– 'Cords consisting of serpents,' according to Kulluka
(Pasaih sarpa-rajjughih). The winkings of men's eyes
Are all numbered by him; he wields the universe
As gamesters handle dice. These are the unexampled days
Of false witness – a barbarous regime which gives power over
  life and death
To an oligarchy of brigands and adventurers,
Without security from vexation by irresponsible tyrants,
Without protection of the home against the aggression of
  criminal bands,
Without impartial justice, without dignity.
We are denied all the deepest needs of men who do not wish
To sink to the level of the beasts – condemned
To a life deprived of its salt.

From *The Meeting of the East and the West*

Heine's words remain true: 'Portuguese, Dutchmen, and
  Englishmen
Have brought home from India the treasures in their big ships.
We were only lookers-on. But the spiritual treasures of India
Shall not escape us.' [...]
Yeats has advised young poets to go to the Upanishads,
And a greater interest in Indian thoughts and ideas
Exists nowhere in the world than in my mind [...]

Why

Concerned as I am with the West Highlands and Hebrides
Instantly to my hand is the fact
That the two greatest social and religious reformers
Of modern India – Dayanandi and Gandhi –
Were both born in the small peninsula of Kathiawar.
Gandhi was born at Porbunder.
It is on the sea-coast, jutting out into the sea,
And has all the infinite variety and charm
Of the expanse of ocean around it.
Mists of extraordinary beauty
Constantly rise from the sea
And encompass the land,
The sea itself is usually a brilliant ultramarine
With liquid green where the shoals lie.
The little town where Gandhi was born
Rises almost out of the sea
And becomes a vision of glory at sunrise and sunset
When the slanting rays beat upon it,
Turning its turrets and pinnacles into gold.
Morvi, where Dayanandi was born, lies inland
Not far away from the desolate waste
Of the Rajputana Desert which stretches to the north
Unbroken for hundreds of miles.
The land at Morvi is rocky
And the country is rugged,
The differences of their birthplaces arc clearly seen
In the differences between Dayanandi and Gandhi.
We have Porbunders and Morvis enough
In Scotland: but they produce
No such outstanding characters
As Dayanandi and Gandhi.
Why?

An t-Urr. Coinneach Ros / Rev. Kenneth Ross

Fògradh Cogaidh sna h-Innsean

Cha do sheac a' ghrian ud
no iorghaill nam mìltean beul
fad réis bhliadhnachan
m' aisling òrdha.

Chuir duathar nam beann sgleò
air iomdhath nan làithean
's allt a' Ghlinne ri crònan
an grunnd mo shaoghail.

'Torwood' a' seinn tro chilltean Bhenàres
's manadh Healabhail air Nanga Pàrbat.

Wartime Exile in India

Neither that sun
nor the cacophony of thousands of mouths
throughout a span of years
withered my golden dream.

The mountains' shade obscured
the kaleidoscope of the days
while the burn of the Glen chattered
in the riverbed of my world.

'Torwood' sounding through the temples of Benares
and the spectre of Healaval on Nanga Parbat.

Edwin Morgan

Dom Raja

If you cannot get your dead to burn,
if the wood will not take, and they are still there
accusing you mornings, evenings after,
if battering rain blurs the flame,
your work spent out in profitless smoke,
if your poverty cannot even steal
matches and oil, among the many waiting
to deliver ranks of other dead,
and flies seethe where fire should,
making the eyes move again and signal
they have an indomitable reproach
for you as you stand alive in the sun:
I will put an end to this if you call for me,
I promise I will make ashes if you need me,
I will leave your accuser without a tongue
if you can pay me, and if you believe
that I know the dead and their ways
and am their king.

I tell you they are not easy to destroy,
the dead. Sometimes with a rush they are back,
circling the camp relentlessly mourning
those that are dead to them, for you
are never as remorseless as they are,
they have no bread to bake or clothes
to wash or anything but time
to fill, and swarming through the bounds
they fall on you, they tear you, eat you,
spit you out to your terror as lacking
the substance they must have. The substance
they must have is not in you and can

never be, so why do they devour you?
I can tell you they are not unappeasable
if you will ask me to tell you. I could show you
how to harrow the little hell they march from
if you were good to me, a little.
You have only to take me aside
to see my kingdom.

Look how I have pushed the broken thing like an ark
burning straight down roaring to the water-line.
I dance, I am set on a throne, my torch
is never out. My suppliants put stones
on the bodies against jackals, and run
to search for me, they scuffle and pray
and ask me to melt their guilt to drops
of fat. The dead smell me far off.
I wrestle with them until they are black.
The Ganges reaches darkly seaward.
Look where I point: the smouldering riches
drift foul and slow, then rough and swift,
still fighting, still twisting towards the living,
still throwing indignations like anchors
to scrape and scour the frowning grief
that lines the banks. The dead are so restless
that even I have to drive them before me
with all my power, but if you want me to do so
– and how few there are who want me to do so –
I will keep them silent, weltering
at the feet of their king.

From 'Planet Wave'

Juggernaut (1600 AD)

I had had enough of stars and silence.
It was midsummer, and I made for India.
Where would I get some life but India?
I joined a boat, and was soon blistering
across the Bay of Bengal to a seaside town
of some fame, what was it called, Puri,
yes, Puri of the festivals. A test case
I was told. Test of what? Oh you'll find out.

If I wanted people, there were plenty of them,
tens, hundreds of thousands, filling the streets
with chatter and movement and colour and slowly
making a magnet of the courtyard of a temple
where they clustered jostling in ancient expectation.
With a rumble, with shouts, with drums, with blowing of shells
an enormous cart rolled out, what, sixteen wheels,
a car for a god, a car for the people to draw,
and draw it they did, with their god on board,
that giant tottering legless fearsome one
they dragged as if drugged, they were high on devotion,
milling, chanting, pushing, stumbling, trundling –
trundling what, on those great spokes, to the sea?
I can hear the roar even yet, mounting up
through waves of heat and dust, it could curdle blood
or it could twine your roots with the roots of the world.
'Who is Lord of the Universe? Jagannath!
Who is Jaganath? Lord of the Universe!'

The juggernaut rolled on, and made its path
over so many bodies no one could say
who had been shouldered to the ground
or who had shouldered themselves to the ground,
embracing the relentless axle of the divine.
I could not say. I did not want to say.
Shining eyes, shouts of ecstasy,
stench, stampede, shattered shinbones,
sun-splashed awnings, sweat-soaked idols
swam before me like sharks, like shrieks
from an old incomprehensible abyss.

The axle squeals without redress of grease.

Tessa Ransford

With gratitude to India

I was a baby in India
born among dark eyes and thin limbs
handled by slim fingers
bounced by bangles
and held high among the turbans,
surrounding by the light sari
black knot of hair
suggestion of spice,
wrapped up only by those songs
that spiral the spirit out of the dust
and lay it down again to sleep.

I crawled among bright toenails
ticked off ants by the gross
or touched the lizard in his cold quickness;
toddled past wilting bougainvillaea
to watch hoopoos on the mai-dan,
caught flashes of minivet, oriole and bulbul
and peered up into huge flowers
on tree after tree
as I broke into their shade.

Never left with a strange
babysitter
I was part of the parties, parades,
the bazaar,
could swallow the stenches and listen
to the poetry of bargaining;
heart's desire was to drink cool water
or chew a sugar-cane
and flap off the flies.

I had dysentery, sickness, paleness
boiled buffalo milk,
no welfare vitamins, no plastic pants.
The sun was a fiend, the rain was a friend
the stars only just out of reach.

Expressions were always changing:
a smile latent in sorrow
and a love in anger;
tears happened with laughter
but patience presided over every mood.

To have first found the world
in abundant India
is my life's greatest privilege.

The dhobi's dog

The dhobi's dog will return from riverbank in the sun
to the house, but not lie down; to and fro he'll trot
panting, semi-wild, hither and thither recalled,
never petted, fondled, either hot or cold.
Does he belong? To whom? Dhobi-ji sends him home,
Bibi-ji won't give him room. Such is my lot.

Born and reared in India, comforted by ayah
on some cool verandah of lofty bungalow
with charpai and degchi, decanter and serahi,
enervated, dusty, the whining mosquito,
black ants and red, huge fans overhead:
when all was done and said, the British had to go.

In Scotland I froze: hands, feet, nose,
in thick uneasy clothes at dour boarding school:
a wind-resistant, dismal, stern, redoubtable,
grey-stone-wall life exemplified by rule;
embarrassed to embrace, weep, laugh, kiss:
was I of this race? from such a gene pool?

I lived in Pakistan, land of the Mussulman,
governed by the Koran. I learnt Punjabi,
dressed in shalwar, travelled to Lahore,
joined in zabur, lived on dal-chapati:
but didn't my passport say 'British, born Bombay'
however long my stay in Sialkot or Karachi?

I like the way I speak, the voice my thoughts make,
yet Scottish folk are quick to think me English.
I've lived here (sixty) years (Anderson forebears
and Glasgow Macalisters – that's buksheesh!)
Still my language finds no place, no ethnic dress or face:
I plead my special case and thus I finish.

My Indian self

Let me be
myself my
Indian self
that goes to extremes
from garland to ashes
Himalaya to desert
mango to maize

Let me wear the silks
the sandals and the gold.
Let me dip my fingers
in the bowl of desire
even here in the puritan
corners of my dwelling

Let me reclaim
myself; I cannot
be curtailed;
extravagance is my form
not my style;
intensity is how
my pulse is rated

My body is myself
however ageing;
I love the way it has borne
with me all these years
and given nothing less
than life itself to others

Happiness is tropical and
love is a house with wide verandahs.
Joy is my element:

I pass it through the test
of water, fire, air
and bring it back to earth

Two way

I think of India and yearn for my childhood,
my parents brave and hardworking who wilted
there, my siblings who died. Here I found
a country reserved as if promised and jilted.

How could I go back now? I made a craft
to sail through the world built from books
of poetry. A flimsy vessel, it stays afloat
through storm and piracy, between the rocks.

That's how my ancestor sailed in a paddle steamer
from Clyde to Malay, became Harbour Master.
Practical, kind, principled, tough, yet prey
to ideals, we're set to go on like that: two way.

Faded Indian bedspread

My faded Indian bedspread
threadbare and washed out
I would not exchange
for a luxurious quilt

With ancient flowering pattern
and cotton endurance
to another generation
its workaday presence

Going nowhere

Travelling to Kashmir
the delectable mountains
five days journey
through the burning plains

At Delhi a telegram
her little girl was ill
she turned back home
turned away from the hills

And I see those who give
up on promised lands
turn back because they have
the present on their hands

The Passenger

I came to the banks of the Lethe
and approached the ferryman:
I asked how much he charged
for a single, no return

I looked across the river
as it rippled in the breeze
then stepped into the rowing-boat
as he took up the oars

Your fare, he said, for crossing
in this weather, on this night
is your last drawn breath
and your last eye-light

Will you take a poem instead:
I have one in my throat?
but it swelled there choking
with wads of paper notes

My blood it is the stream
my breath it is the wind
my body forms the boat
for the ferryman: my mind

The dreams I have

The dreams I have are all of the dead
my mother and father who never fail
to encompass me wherever I'm led

The husband who loved my poems and read
them with often a believing smile
comforts my dreams although now dead

The kindly woman from Wazirabad
who helped me when the children were small
is often around wherever I'm led

Long-ago friends and Vera who fed
my mind and heart with talk and tale
appear in my dreams despite being dead

It seems as if they are free and glad
to emerge as if in answer to call
and encompass me wherever I'm led.

Jane Bhandari

Steel Blue

1

The sea under rain-clouds
Was blued steel,
And the black boats
Flying orange and magenta flags,
Cut silver streaks in the blue.
A white line of rain
Divided the islands from the sea.
The sea milk-white
The sea dark blue
The sea carved by boats
Into silver scimitars against the dark.
The lighthouse rising
Out of the dark and woolly blue,
The horizon a blue line,
The far islands clear and blue,
Then fainter, diminished by mist,
But still blue.

2

I have not enough blue
To describe the boats
Canopied in bright cobalt
Against the drenching rain:
The big water-tank of the harbour
Also bright blue, to signify holding water,
And the sky shot with the burnished blue
Of heated steel. *Watch*, my father said:

At a certain temperature, the steel
Colours straw, then blue, and finally,
Black. Nothing will change it back.
And I, watching the glowing steel
Of the clock hands being blued,
Understood the significance
Of an irreversible change. That change
Was magical, the silver changing to straw,
And suddenly flashing iridescent blue
That became the navy of a raven's wing.

3

The polished steel of the sea darkens
To the colour of the alchemist's stone,
Brushed by the cold fire of sky,
And shadowed by clouds
Walking tip-toe across water
Blue as the steel; small islands
Floating densely, hard little rocks
Suspended from a shifting horizon.
A sky pillowed with clouds
And shot with blue:
Against the sky, birds scatter blue
Into the sea from their wings
With every shift and turn,
Carve their own scimitar lines in the air
Above the boats that cut
Through the steel-hard sea:
The effort palpable below, but above
The lines cut effortlessly
Into the blue, glance off the billows
Of the cotton-wool cloud pillows
Foaming along the horizon.
Blue, too, in windows reflecting sky,

And one tall building, the glass building
Full of sky, broken by other buildings,
This too, blue, and blue, and blue.

4

I have run out of blue.
But the alchemist sky
Still transmutes the sea
Into blue steel, dented by sun,
Then wiped out by rain,
A wet sponge leaving only
A blank page, emptiness,
Soft whiteness wiping across the steel blue:
But when clouds darken the water
After the sky has fallen into it,
And the horizon
Advances and retreats with the rain,
The sea is the alchemist of the sky,
Transmuting colour and time.

5

My father prepared the whitely shining steel,
Rubbing it till it shone like a cloud,
A soft sheeny white that belied the steel.
The blue suddenly spread across
Like a jay's wing, a peacock's tail,
The alchemy of heat on steel
Transmuting the cloud-white sheen
To the dark intense blue of the sea under sun.

6

I wish not for the unchanging blue of the steel,
But for the possibility of change: to reflect
The blue of the sky within my waters,
And change as the sea changes, eternally.
The little boats are tethered to the shore
By invisible strings, returning endlessly to the land,
Like young goats to their mother.
Thus I return to my old haunts, drawn
By those invisible threads casting a spider's web
Across half the world, their pull as strong
As the strongest rope, but as delicate
As the spider's thread, and as sticky –
They do not let go easy, each pull is pain,
Taking me back to my childhood
To parents, to old loves, to children, again
Back to old memories I would rather forget.
But I remember: unwilling, I remember
The child that went far away,
But always returned to the memory of blue.

The clock-hands were set in place.
The clock was wound.
Time moved along blued-steel tracks,
Around and around.

Chrys Salt

Flight (The Himalayas 1959)

'We must go now. We must go now,
 we must go now,' my father said.
'The iron bird flies, their horses come on wheels!'

And from the savage tenor of the times,
I learn how frost can gobble noses,
blizzards bite, snow blind, and mountains fall,

how men will stalk us with their guns,
across the frozen halls of dark,
our tears and cries too loud for secrecy,

how small and sudden is goodbye,
how hope and terror weigh the same,
how many ways there are to die.

How when the moon is bright we'll hide,
or hand in hand stumble down broken stairs of night.
How tombs of snow will follow us,

men fall like boulders down ravines,
shoes shred, cold burn and friends betray.
How when one dies we will not stop or grieve.

How I will see my dad piss arcs of blood,
a crimson poppy blossoming in snow.
How still he'll carry me like faith

through air as thin as prayer and skin,
past roaring cataracts, down slithering rock,
careful as sacred culture on his back.

How when we cross to safety in this land,
I'll find a tiny patch of flowers like stars,
nuzzled in a barren cleft of stone.

How I will offer dad my sad bouquet,
and place it gently in his ruined hands.
How he will take me in glad arms and weep.

Note:
Following the failed Tibetan uprising against Chinese religious
suppression in 1959, the Delhi Llama fled across the Himalayas
to find refuge and political asylum in India. Many thousands of
Tibetan refugees followed him into permanent exile by the same
treacherous route.

Refuge (Darjeeling 2016)

Balls in their colour coded wool store,
glow like sun-struck apples in a loft.
Madder root, walnut husk and indigo.

Bent fingers with long memories,
tease wool and card industriously.
Feet that have climbed through ice and sky,
tread makeshift spinning wheels.
No one looks up, they have their work to do.

Others, perhaps their daughters, crouch on stools,
bend to the clatter clunk of looms,
the bang of mallets, patter of young feet.
Phoenix and dragon climb the warp,
with cranes, mandalas,
snow-lions, lotus-flowers.

Out of the blue, one asks how old I am.
Taken aback, I tell her, show off,
pirouette on one leg like a dancer.
Lacking a common language, play the fool.
Then she says through an interpreter,
'Old women walk like this in our culture,'
crooks her back, hobbles across the floor,
mimes toothlessness to gales of laughter.

Note: The Tibetan Refugee Centre, Darjeeling is a self-supporting
rehabilitation centre for Tibetan refugees in the Darjeeling
Himalayan hill region. It was founded in 1959 after they followed
The Delhi Llama and escaped from Tibet, after the Chinese
invasion. The production of Tibetan handicraft, especially carpets, is
the Centre's main activity.

Grand Hotel, Kolkata

Our tea is brought,
in china thin as fingernails.
Fragrant Darjeeling,
with fruitcake jewelled with cherries,
cucumber sandwiches, thin-sliced,
triangular.

Orbs of lamplight fruit
from ornamental poles,
illuminate the baize of courtyard lawns,
the pristine tablecloths,
glint on the silver plated cutlery,
the turquoise pool
where night time bathers bask and loll
like river fish.

And here we are sipping delicious tea,
moneyed, elegant and insular,
talking of NGOs, the rural poor,
how to cure the ills of India.

Beyond a cool and pillared entrance hall,
Sikh doormen in their skirted robes, tall
ceilings with colonial cornices,
the wheezing of a punkhawallah's rope
is scarcely audible.

Punkhawallah

Campanologist of air.
Patient rope-tugger.
Whoosher of charpai.
Wafter of verandah.
Heat juggler. Outsider.

He is stone deaf this one,
chosen for silent trustworthy discretion.
Under the gutter's stink, heat
heaves from earth and stuccoed walls.
Sweat drips in dust
too hot for naked feet.
A rope loops round a swollen toe
passes through a hole
to axle and pulley in the bungalow.

All within is cool and confidential.
Domestic argument. Military discussion.
The sahib sucks his pipe,
leafs through last season's Punch,
volumes of Government reports and letters.

Memsahib oversees
ayah and dhobi, dressing boy and cook,
grumbles how indolent the servants are.
Writes to her mother.

Hour upon hour, his chest caves in and out,
mimics the heavy wheezing of the punkha.
And none will know his name
but 'punkhawallah',
his inky thumb print in the master's ledger.

Glossary:
punkha – a fan, especially a large swinging screen like fan hung
from the ceiling and operated by a servant.
charpai – a traditional Indian bedstead of woven webbing or hemp,
stretched on a wooden frame.

Ian Brown

Calcutta/Kolkata, January 2012

In 1910 the Editor
Of Scottish Churches College Calcutta Magazine
Wrote 'seeing it has pleased God
To link together the destinies
Of India and Great Britain,
We shall give our ungrudging allegiance
To our new Sovereign, King George the Fifth'
And mourned a blow that fell with 'startling suddenness':
'Before almost we knew of his danger,
Our Emperor had passed beyond
The gates of death.'

'Edward the Peacemaker' sits astride
His monumental horse at an approach
To his mother's whited marble monument.
Diametrically opposite that main avenue
On which she sits enthroned,
R. I., Queen-Empress,
And he, Rex Imperator, placed by God,
Was then mourned in Calcutta.

In Kolkata now the monument shines at midday
And subtly shifts shade in dusk's fading light,
The gardens trimmed, the walks maintained,
The flower beds neat as in English gardens
When – once – 'England' could mean 'Britain'
And 'Empire' seemed God's dispensation
To the Empire-makers.

In this Kolkata dusk, empire is colonised,
Resumed, absorbed, retrieved by couples
Walking hand-in-hand in their India.
Children run, families stroll,
Appropriating the royal-imperial appropriations,
Ensuring their monument is now theirs
And, de-alienated, domesticated,
No symbol of God's dispensation,
Now newly conceived, newly enjoyed,
Not rejected,
Its meaning transformed.

A tourist in Bishnupur

In the terracotta temple town,
Massive ceremonial sites and monumental gateways
Open your eyes – and mind – to what is here
Taken for granted, to visitors revelation.

The Modan Mohan Temple's facades pique
The mind and eyes with plaque after plaque
Detailing the Ramayana, Krishna's life and love,
Radha's devotion to him, his to her.

Respect kept me out the temple's heart,
But, circulating round, the building's images lifted my
spirit:
One showed Krishna encountering a water monster,
Finely detailed, beautifully expressive.

It made me think for a moment
Of Columba and the Loch Ness Monster,
But such a parallel at once seemed glib,
Trying to appropriate what's powerful – akin, but distinct.

Maps

In the Second World War, it is said,
A Sikh soldier escaped through Burma
From the Japanese.

He told intelligence officers
He had navigated all the way
Using a map he had hidden.

When they asked to see the map,
He handed over, carefully preserved,
A diagrammatic map of the London Underground.

On it he had encoded his journey,
His left turnings, his right turnings,
His straight aheads.

We all, I suppose, use what maps
We think we have to work out
Our way through life.

And, whatever reality our maps relate to,
We cherish the truth we think
They hold for us.

Driving in India

The sign says 'Obey the traffic law'
The notice says 'Obey traffic rules'

The meaning: 'Sauve qui peut'
The rule: *Anything goes*

Sheena Blackhall

Lament for the Raj

Mither's Uncle Dougie, an faither's Cousin John –
Ane vrocht in Kuala Lumpur – the tither in Ceylon;
Twa hin-hochs o the Raj's rump … the tail-eyn o its reign
Milkin siller ooto rubber trees – the Fite Man's gravy-train.

Atap ma mither's mantle (Dougie's gift frae Singapore)
An ebon elephant wad raxx its muckle chouks an roar.
Three monkeys cocked abune the press: ane's lugs frae lees war
  stappit;
Anither's mou wis steekt frae ill; the hinmaist's een war happit;
An ben the hearth, on box o braisse, far granny's coal wis keepit,
Emblazoned wis a tiger, creepin forrit, fly an sleekit.

Johnny's keepsake? Twa braid oxen rugged a braisse cairt wi a reef
As princely's a pagoda, fit fur Rajah or Caliph.
In the firelicht o an evenin, foo yon oriental breets
Wided ben a bairnie's fancies, far the Real an Unreal meets!

Mither's Uncle Dougie, an faither's Cousin John
O Aiberdeenshire fairmin stock, war eident an won on;
Two sahibs brocht up on sowens, cheengin kail fur vindaloo,
Spikkin Hindi melled wi Doric on the roads frae Katmundu –
Oh, the schule buiks fu o mahouts an mongooses that I read!
Foo I yearned tae cross the coolie lines far Jumbos trumpeted!
Tae converse wi haly Saddhus, dusky Brahmins, warlike Sikhs
In the jungles an the temples far the slit-ee'd cobra keeks!

Mither's Uncle Dougie, an faither's Cousin John –
The nearest tae their Eastern airts I reached wis Foggieloan.
Noo my quinie's pulse is quickened bi the TV's trashy trock –
Foo she yearns tae gyang tae Disneyland (the thocht o't gars
  me bock)
Viewin Mickey Moose an Donald, ettin Super Macs an Cokes
Or tae traivel tae Australia, the surf-lan o the Soaps!

Thoombnail Theology

Yahweh an Kali –
Hell's richt up their alley;
Like them I canna ...
My deid-end's Nirvana

Krishna an Allah –
Twa wheels, the same barra;
Foo pit a face on
Cosmic creation?

I force-feed
Nae Godheid
Gie my seed
Nae wersh creed
Nae deus
In my hoose
Nae papoose
In guilt's noose
Karma an Dhyana
(Born ootside the toga)
Are my moral guidelines
As siccar as tramlines.

Consumer-expressed
Buddhist is best!

Christine de Luca

Meeting India for the first time

Closest I ever got to you was watching
a lissom Indian dancer. After the drama
of the Scots girls with their kilted kicking,
then clicking Irish feet and stair-rod arms,
her body flowed delight, without a sound.
As she turned, it seemed she conjured birds
mysterious from trees; a story grounded,
pre-verbal, beyond the need of words.

She hid from view the endless repetition,
the strain of learning every tiny movement.
It seemed a gift she opened for our pleasure,
an invitation. There was no partition
of spirit or of mind from body. Barefoot,
she danced us back into a youthful future.

As I turned fae a ATM machine

a camel cam stoorin by, pooin a kert.
He luikit doon his nose at me i da wye
at only a camel can, for I wis gawpin

at him, at his stately neck wi hits paintit
swastika for aa ta see. Summonin
da wisdom o his forbears, he seemed ta say

'dis symbol brings luck, göd healt an strent,
an maks da sun sheen waarm apön you,
helps you fin love, wealt, final liberation!'

He wis fair pinnin alang, yon camel
wi da swastika apön his neck, bördly-lik,
wi a muckle lod, nae budder ava.

stoorin: *moving swiftly;* pooin: *pulling;* kert: *cart;* göd: *good;* pinnin:
moving swiftly; bördly-lik: *robust-looking;* lod: *load;* budder:
bother; ava: *at all*

Note: The swastika in India is an ancient symbol which has strong
positive connotations. The Nazis subverted this symbol, reversing it
in the process.

Fire – Sang Cycle

Shetland and Rajastan

Da first notes

A göd paet bank is een
wi deep moor, a third paet,
blue at da boddom, nae
horse-fleysh ta speak o,
a dry hill for kerryin,
an a loch tae guddle in.

A göd hoose has,
aroond da door,
twartree buffalo
for lassi an for mylk
an sharn. Forbye,
dey'll poo da ploo.

Da wye gifts lie aroond wir feet,
maistlins we foryet ta luik.

Finnin da harmony

Ripper an flayer,
rhythm o tushkar,
pattern o paetbank;
wind wark an sun wark.
Raise dem an roog dem,
borrow-foo, kishie-foo,
dem,
hurl dem, rin wi dem,
dem,
a saeson's wark half dön.
dön.

Hent aa da sharn,
tagelia head-heich,
mix hit wi strae,
flatsh aa da uple;
lay dem ta dry,
raise dem an roog

lift dem an kerry

a saeson's wark half

Da wye hit sings i wir blöd,
but we dunna laek hits tön.
Makkin da sang

Da wye da steid is set,
waa biggit, clods shöled,
haert bluest an best,
trim tae da tap;
a faelly röf.

Da steid set richt, uple biggit,
raa apön raa, dis wye an
dat wye, peerie roond biggins,
taps graftit aff;
fine an dry.

Da wye a faemly is beelt,
shapit, shaltered, luikit tae.

Completin da sang cycle

I da greff, faels
an skyumpies laid
sae dey can bed doon
inta new laand.

Uple for da fire,
ess for cleanin;
whit's owre höved
back tae da göd aert.

Da wye we come inta dis wirld,
ös hit an, tipperin, laeve hit.

lassi: yoghurt; *tagelia:* multi-purpose metal basins usually carried on the head; *uple:* fuel pats made from dung and straw

göd: *good;* paet: *peat;* blue: *dense peat;* horse-fleysh: *fibrous peat;* twartree: *a few;* sharn: *dung;* forbye: *besides;* poo: *pull;* ploo: *plough;* tushkar: *special peat-cutting spade;* roog: *build in heaps;* kishie: *cane or straw basket for the back;* hurl: *trundle in barrow;* hent: *gather;* flatsh: *flatten;* blöd: *blood;* tön: *tune;* steid: *foundation;* shöled: *shovelled;* faelly: *turf;* röf: *roof;* raa: *row;* peerie: *little;* biggins: *structures;* greff: *ditch (at base of peat bank);* skyumpies: *large turf blocks;* ess: *ash;* höved: *heaved;* ös: *use;* tipperin: *unable to set foot down*

Aa but carbon neutral
Jaipur 2009

A man sits at his table i da street,
lifts a haevy iron fae a sunbaked tile.

Lasses crubbit in a rickshaa,
der saris eclipse da bougainvillea.

I da haert o a roondaboot, twartree tents;
women hing oot washin, day laaberers.

A midder traivels peeriewyes;
a airm o a tree balanced apön her head.

Anidder wi a lod o laeves:
her goat has a short tedder.

Bruck bi da roadside waeled trowe;
recycled bi a stray dog, a antrin coo.

aa but: *almost;* crubbit: *restricted for space;* twartree: *a few;*
laaberers: *labourers;* midder: *mother;* traivels: *walks;* peeriewyes:
slowly; anidder: *another;* lod: *load;* tedder: *tether;* bruck: *rubbish;*
waeled trowe: *sifted through;* antrin: *occasional;* coo: *cow*

Blending in
In recognition of 50 years for the Singh family in Edinburgh

Edinburgh was a cold host half a century ago
for the tailor from Amritsar; a grey place
for a Sikh who had looked on a golden temple.

There are three generations of Singhs now
to stir warmth into this stern outpost:
twenty families listed in the phone directory.

Dressed in tartan, they all assemble
to celebrate their several identities; a unique
blend of Sikh and Scottish cultures.

The spread prepared has a heady aroma
Chinese, Italian, Indian cuisine
with a pièce de résistance in haggis pakora.

They line up for the family photo, swathed
in their new tartan. The kilt looks good on them
and the twist of matching tartan in their turbans.

What would the old man have made of this,
the tailor? Would he have laughed or cried
or criticised the weave, the stitching?

He would have seen the colours of beloved flags
in a sway of pleats: green, gold, blue, orange
hot hues of India, of the Punjab, disciplined

to the Campbell tartan – the one in which
Sikh regiments marched curtly to the tune
of British monarchs. A second glance down

the Singh column in the phone directory reveals
new city threads to blend in: a swatch of names,
of new histories to tartan Edinburgh.

Alan Spence

Ganesha

I'm not an animal, I'm not a man,
I am a god – I Am since time began.
God of Beginnings, Guardian at the Gate,
I'm Lord of Thresholds, transcend time and fate.

What you see is the form that I assume.
Here I am, the elephant in the room –
proboscis, tusks, pot belly, flapping ears.
Light on my feet, I'll dance away your fears.

Ganesha, Remover of Obstacles,
performer of everyday miracles.
Your children know me well, each avatar –
I'm Horton, Dumbo, Kala Nag, Babar.

But yes, those obstacles – who put them there?
Now, offer me your mantra, homage, prayer.
Aum Ganeshaya Nama – chant my name.
Aum Ganeshaya Nama – chant my name.

John Purser

Râg Shri in Glasgow
For Prakriti Dutta

It is the rich dark opening in the belly of your voice
which first alerts me to the danger I am in,
so visceral my whole skin primps itself
without command.

Around us, the huge deserted studio, empty
save for packing cases, a single chair,
a grand piano and its stool,
transforms into a heat-haze over desert plains;
far beyond, green forest rises into snow-capped peaks
higher than the clouds.

As your voice gently explores its middle range,
leaving blossoms trailing from every wall
and the floor strewn with petals,
the aroha of the râg rises, yearning,
your tongue as though in search of moisture
although moist itself. 'It is like,' you say,
'meeting with your lover. You really don't unfold yourself,
but you also want to show your beauty: so you can always feel
a hidden beauty inside this râg melody.'

All this blends like a miracle with
the sinuous line in Erik Chisholm's
Hindustani Concerto: the same râg rises
as a rippling ostinato breaks upon the shores
of his exotic music in gentle, urgent waves, until it all subsides
into a beautiful submission to, admission of
irresistible desire.

When you were here, you left behind
a little colourful Hindu god, legs folded,
mouth with serious expression
concentrating on his hands held out
clashing his cymbals. He is seated
on a window ledge and still protects the house
with loyal concentration.

But he is not as strong as your absence,
and your voice still travels through my being
from a land I've never seen; will never see.

Liz Lochhead

Something I'm Not

familiar with, the tune
of their talking, comes tumbling before them
down the stairs which (oh I forgot) it was my turn
to do again this week.
My neighbour and my neighbour's child. I nod, we're not
on speaking terms exactly.

I don't know much about her. Her dinners smell
different. Her husband's a busdriver,
so I believe.
She carries home her groceries in Grandfare bags
though I've seen her once or twice around the corner
at Shastri's shopping for spices and such.
(I always shop there – he's open till all hours
making good). How does she feel?
Her children grow up with foreign accents,
swearing in fluent Glaswegian. Her face
is sullen. Her coat is drab plaid, hides
but for a hint at the hem, her sari's
gold embroidered gorgeousness. She has
a jewel in her nostril.
The golden hands with the almond nails
that push the pram turn blue
in the city's cold climate.

Valerie Gillies

Tipu's Amulet in Edinburgh Castle

He wore it on his upper arm, next his skin,
so there must be something in it.
He fastened the talisman of destiny to him,
never to be taken off. At the storming
of the fort, finding Tipu's body still warm,
Captain Young untied it from his arm.

Sewn up in flowered silk, a bubble
of brittle metal is hidden from sight.
With its Arabic manuscript, the flat capsule
slides around as if alive, inside.
The blowers on knots chant powerful words,
musk in the ink and a sharp Persian sword.

Given to wear with love, no amulet
is a piece of dead matter, cold, inert.
How many times can it protect? Two
musket-balls passed through his chainmail shirt.
A stolen amulet, losing its active powers,
can withhold them from its new owner.

Overgrown with jungle, the old Gajalhatti Pass
still shows what's called *Tipu's Road* in places.
His amulet harms no-one. The angel's writing
is shut up among crowded gems in glass cases.
This is one relic which can restore
a hero, a future, to the state of Mysore.

Seringapatam, Mysore State

At first, I heard the story from their side.
With Muslim friends on motorbikes
I went to Srirangaputtana for a picnic.
We were students wandering through the fortress,
Hearing it all, the whole citadel on an island,
The sultan no-one could beat, so warlike
He dressed his troops in tiger stripes:
The Tiger of Mysore, our Tipu
Holding off the British, a national hero.
Then the traitor vizier opened a secret passage
And let the enemy in, that judas!

When Tipu was killed, an electric storm
Struck British officers where they stood.
His sons were taken captive, all four,
To make way for the old Raja of Mysore.
They passed through the gate on elephants:
Each boy had a sprig of pearls in his turban
And round his neck an emerald of great size,
With strings of rubies and brilliants.

It seemed impregnable, the fort,
They were up against a bend, a steep slope.
'Why did we wash that fruit in the river?
I think I'm shaking with some fever.'
The back of Ahwad's hand on my forehead:
'No, you're walking where the British put their dead.'
We built a fire on the riverbank. Taking a drum,
The nightwatchman sang a ballad of Tipu Sultan.
Abandoned citadel, deep in the mofussil,
The drumbeat and the sound of jackals.
And in me, a horror of its scorched grass,
The slope, the breach, the sense of loss.

A year later, back at home: 'Srirangaputtana?
Thon's the battle o Seringapatam,'
Said Granfaither, 'I've aye thocht
It was whaur your great grand uncle focht,
I hae his cartouche bag and powder horn.
They met wi the braw tiger troops haun tae haun,
In the river an up the brae, wi mony deid.
The heilanders played the pipes in the breach.'

What She Told Her Friend
*A variation on the classic Tamil love poem by Venmaniputti,
a woman poet of the first century AD*

At a late-night party watched by no-one
who had not been drinking,
in sofas like groves
filled with leaves and birdsong,
on the banks of chintz
clustered with flowers,

I sat in his lap

my arm around his neck
My eyes could not see him

 it was too smoky

and he got too close
my ears could not hear him

full of his kisses

and snaps of laughter
But my hand grew beautiful
on his shoulder
and shrivelled to bone
when I took it away

What am I to make of this?

The Black Bike

Wearer of a blue Afghan turban
above magnificent features,
he kept on the old warlike look.

He became my best friend.
He'd made up his mind about that
when we met, riding on the racecourse.

Changing from horse to motorbike
gives the balance a queer turn.
My knees had to stop gripping.

For a year we roamed the south
on the black Norton together,
my crash-helmet an oven.

We saw the mosque from the outside
and that field where a Parsee pulled
my father from the fiery wreck in '42.

Yes, I had a great view of India:
it was all your broad back, Manzoor,
and villagers waving to the black bike.

Ruby Tiger Land

They live in ruby tiger land.
Hers the stroke that slays,
hers the sun that draws
and devours live eyesight.

Moth-dusk evenings
swag the peacocks in royal blue
from tree to tree in India,
cry their evening cry:

miaou-aou-aou,
companion to the tiger.
He gives his ruby roar
In the sallow grasses below.

He flames steady flame,
not black-ash like the boar
who bristles among roots,
shows his scoriated tushes.

A sambhur buck starts and bugles.
Feel the presentiment of game,
the knowledge that they are close by
before you see them.

Why do you do them this way,
land? – you hill goddess
with rubied eyepits, and coated in
the many colours of rosewood forest.

Patriot

Nadir, Nadir Shah
leaves the forest
where he lay
concealed.

And is he new?

In change of mind's possession,
blue-ribbed his breastcage,
feathered his heart's
whud and banged flapping.

And is he winged?

Flack-flacking across the treetops
he comes out to deliver his country,
flying turquoise as a shoal of parrots
airborne by their own fierce jibes.

Fellow Passenger

Mister B Rajan, diamond buyer,
crystallises from this travelling companion.
He goes by rail, it seems, by criss
and cross, Hyderabad to Bangalore
to Madras, Madras, Madras,
seeking the industrial diamond.

He brings new orient gems from hiding.
Himself, he wears goldwealthy rings
of ruby, and, for fortune,
another of God Venkateswaran.
His smile is a drillpoint diamond's,
incisive his kindness.

Sparrowboned, he walks unstable passageways,
living on boiled eggs and lady's-fingers
with noggins of whisky to follow.
He dreams of his house, the shrineroom picture
of Sai Baba, corkscrew-haired young saint.
And he has at home beautiful hidden daughters.

The Piano-tuner

Two hundred miles, he had come
    to tune one piano, the last hereabouts.
Both of them were relics of imperial time:
    the Anglo-Indian and the old knockabout.

He peered, and peered again
    into its monsoon-warped bowels.
From the flats of dead sound he'd beckon
    a tune on the bones out to damp vowels.

His own sounds were pidgin.
    The shapeliness of his forearms
lent his body an English configuration,
    but still, sallow as any snakecharmer

he was altogether piebald.
    Far down the bridge of his nose
perched roundrimmed tortoiseshell spectacles;
    his hair, a salt-and-pepper, white foreclosed.

But he rings in the ear yet,
    his interminable tapping of jarring notes:
and, before he left,
    he gave point to those hours of discord.

With a smile heavenly
    because so out of place, cut off from any home there,
he sat down quietly
    to play soft music: that tune of 'Beautiful Dreamer',

a melody seized from yellowed ivories
    and rotting wood. A damper
muffled the pedal point of lost birthright, We eaves-
    dropped on an extinct creature.

Trick of Memory

Three years north
of the tropic of Cancer
have changed me.
I no longer put oil on my head
or sew jasmine, to sleep with it in my hair.
I pinch shut the letters from India:
it is difficult to picture their writer,
crosslegged on a teak swing indoors.

I used to long for a pair
of the silver toe-rings worn by women
married into the princely family.
Now their faint sound would seem
unattainable as a skein of geese.
I used to love the royal blue
of the two-tone sun-and-shade
silk sari worn by the mothers
of pretty boys named Dilip or Ajoy.
Now that blue would seem
remote as a piece of sky.
I do not care to remember
what husband would entitle me to toe-rings,
or what son would have sent me peacock saris.

Haiku from India

Remember the path
through tall leafy trees at Hassan –
casuarinas?

> Out of the forest
> thoughts start up –
> spotted deer

A bullock cart
with a cheetah on board
in blackbuck country

> Lieutenant Bijly:
> his name means 'lightning',
> his horse is Spitfire

Deep in the forest
stands a great rock:
O, it is a *gaur!*

> A syce waits with
> the borrowed racehorse:
> hooves scatter the gravel

Didn't notice the boy
fasten spurs on boots today?
Time you quit India.

> Promise never to
> cross the *kala pani*, great
> ocean, black water

Vikram Seth

Western Highlands

Across the loch, its surface malachite-pure,
The mist unravels from the farther shore.
I stumble upon a track in the faltering light.
Grey-veiled red deer pause in the stance of flight.

Deb Narayan Bandyopadhyay

Sunday Morning at Castle Rock

Last night I crawled up
The stairs of the ancient, lonely castle
Like a snake coiling up the hidden mysteries
On a moonless light, dark and strange
It all seemed so unreal, magical

The procession of kings
Of shadows:
The Stuarts line up
Spitting tongues of fire in darkness
The great royal icons
Fade out uttering long syllables:
Nemo me impune lascessit
Don't mess with me. I destroy.
Ruins, ravages, dead soldiers
Lie scattered like dead leaves.

I wake up
In the morning at Castle Rock
I look at the domes of the castle,
Bright and glistening
At those strange brave words:
Nemo me impune lascessit.
Don't mess with me. I destroy.

Edinburgh Memories

Stairs climb on to the sky
The sky seemed not the sky
Of the earth
Walter Scott looks on from the monument
Thoughtful, a decorous quill in hand.
Dark unknown crowds far below
Look strange miniatures-
At a standstill
By the magic wand.

The afternoon glow
Grows pendulous, pensive
The faint music of bagpipers
Brings strange, distant feelings
Of being lost, enmeshed.

Lost in the long stretches
Of the Royal Mile
I run past shadows
The Queen from her summer residence peeps out
Smiles from the Holyrood Palace
At the loitering Indian native.

I begin to mutter
Strange words
From the unknown shores
Of the Indian Ocean.

Homage to Jim Alison

Who says Jim is no more?
Wrong,
He journeyed from Scotland to Bankura
Like a cloud, like a wave, like a floating green leaf.

Who says Jim is no more?
Wrong.
He travelled to the Orient
Like a shooting star, like a dream, like a new-born planet.

Who says Jim is no more?
Wrong.
He now moves into the rural spaces
On the hills of green Susunia
Like a breeze, like an ever-flowing fountain, like the mild rain.

Who says Jim is no more?
Wrong.
He flips through the pages of his books in Bankura
Like an unnamed angel, like a mystery, like a fragrance.

There is a knock at the door of the library
 In Bankura
I open the door:
'Welcome home, Jim, my friend!'

Bashabi Fraser

The Same Moon: from Edinburgh to Calcutta: A   Refracted Lens

And what do you discern
When you turn your gaze
From the crystal lights
Of February nights
To return to the dewy days
Of eastern ways?

You are startled by the heron
That you mistake for a gull
As it stilts across the Maidan
Which hasn't seen the fall
That has cast in winter shadows
The verdure of your Meadows.

You wonder how would Outram
Have responded to Gandhi's March
If they had met out on his ghats –
Could such a meeting build an arch
Across the Hoogly – stall the dam
That rose between it and the ramparts

Of Empire? You stroll in dreamy reverie
Recollecting clouds of snow
That clustered round your feathery glow
Jolted by the jagged line
Of towers towering your skyline
So used to Georgian revelry

In granite, masoned to portray
A stolid Highland holding sway
Only to be outdone by hills
That gently push their way
To breathe free and softly feel
Your silvery light, that now
Has skirted the dark brow

Of Arthur's Seat, to encounter the numerous halls
Of the Governor's Palace and its walls
Gleaming, as you race to face
The Gothic splendour of the days
Of High Court's rule. Then it's a leisurely stroll
Round Dalhousie's empty mall
Wondering at the red brick walls
Of Writers' Building, reminiscent
Of your British days.

Do' care

In a Paris hotel lounge on one occasion
My thirteen-year-old five-foot-five
Daughter glowed with the attention
Of three young men striving
To pigeon-hole her Scottishness
And break her brittle brusqueness
With their far-eastern finesse.

If Scotland played England
Whom would she support
– Sco'land – was the answer delivered
And if England played India
– India – she claimed with triumphant swagger.
If England played Germany
– Germany – was the response
From the unassailable position
Of a new-found nationalism.

And what if it were Scotland and India
One demanded with the diabolical confidence
Of an argument-winning lawyer –
She clamped down her glass, shrugged her bare
Shoulders, turned away saying – do' care.

Tartan & Turban

Give me your tartan
And I will imbue it with
The spirit of my race.
I can defend your borders
As I did the Punjab's
In long war-torn days.

I will wear your tartan
With the pride and strength
Of my history and tribe.
I will weave in its pattern
The breadth and length
Of five rivers that subscribed
To my wealth, which I will now
Lend to your tartan
And make it mine – this new
Singh tartan, willing to
Blend with my Sikh turban
At my journey's end.

Paisley

Paisley on your palate
And paisley on your looms
Paisley round your shoulders
And paisley in your rooms
Paisley softening cushions
Paisley brightening rugs
Paisley lacing tables
And ornamenting jugs

Brought from the Kashmir valley
This curious mango shape
Chained out in complex colours
And designs for your landscape.

Transformation by the North Sea

The wind raced across from the North Sea
Through the Meadows to awaken me
To the reality
Of this stormy city.

It unfurled the folds of my sari
Till it billowed out in outraged fury
And I vowed I'd reject its gracious dignity
Till I was in a climate of predictability.

So I have swathed my femininity in denims and coat
My tresses held back by a tea-cosy hat
In a crowd I know that I always stand out
In spite of my accent and tartaned format!

The Affirmation

We were late for church, having struggled
To get our daughter out of bed
On a Sunday morning, which is not an easy task.
And we couldn't pretend that we were casual
Visitors, having lost our way. So instead
Of sauntering through the imposing oak archway
We followed our friend, not daring to ask
Her why she led us on this circuitous route
Round this ivy-straddled edifice, scuttling like freed
Chickens to the closed back door –
To slip us in unnoticed, as she had no doubt
That the congregation's concentration would indeed
Be turned to the minister entering the main door.

We were relieved that we'd made it before
The baptism family was summoned to the fore –
But one kindly lady at the end of our pew
In warm Scottish fashion, turned round to show
Her welcome. As she shook hands, she ventured
'And where are you from?' I answered
'We live here' – indicating somewhere close by,
'Where are you actually from?' she repeated urgently.
The priest began the service, I heard the pride
In my voice as I said 'from India'
Which reassured her; but sparks appeared
In my daughter's eyes – dark and protesting
Drowning my explanation, as they explicitly affirmed
That she was from *here* and not just there.

The Kathak Dancers at the Edinburgh Festival

They stand with their backs to you –
These five in black and red.
They do not come to mesmerise you
With their violet silks or golden muslin.

They come in colours you will recognise
And rhythms that will knock you out
Of your complacence, to be startled by
Their intricacies, their daring, their power!

They count, flicking fingers in this
Bated silence. They turn and strike
Deep in your hearts, setting them beating.

They swirl with abandon, rotating and
Revolving till your head reels
And you lose consciousness
Of differences between east and west
And you don't know that you have stood up
And joined in the deafening applause.

Ragas and Reels

The rollicking rhythm from Highland Springs
Matched with classical ankle bells,
Lifts the mists from burn and brae
Disperses monsoon clouds away
The quick step tunes, with urgency
Spur the dancers to a frenzy
Of hypnotic movement, with precision and verve
Compelling eyes, sharp turns and curves
Mudras like magic, swift wave of hand
Feet beat the tala, challenging the band
The floodlights shower beams, the footlights applaud
This vision of fusion from home and abroad.

The Restauranteur

Corus is the steel bridge
That has spanned across
Continents to bring together
Two nations in a world of
Free enterprise, as Tata
Steps in to keep the furnace aglow.
Metaphors mix, with the red heat
Of metal becoming the slogan
Of curries cooked for the host
Nation to its expectation,
Sold with aplomb by a Bollywood
Star. His name is Khan
And he is no terrorist, but
A Bangladeshi entrepreneur
Whose millions in taxes keep
Scotland's finance alight
With the promise that satisfies
Palates with attractive returns.

Ivy

For me this was the picture of old England
Stolid, Victorian manor houses with unclimbable stone walls
Or tucked away cottages in suburban retreats
Clutched, fondled, smothered, cradled by ivy.
Its dark, green glossy abundance protecting and claiming as its
    own
The grand exteriors, built with commerce from a world
It chose to shut out with a penchant for the privacy of the
    privileged
Assisted by the multiplying fronds of encasing, enveloping ivy.

So when we bought our bungalow – that word reminiscent
Of supervisory edifices of colonial India, dominating
And interrupting forests and tea gardens, hill stations
And river resorts, I saw the ivy peering and peeping at me
Over the garage door and from under a sloping roof
Wondering why I had come from another world
To disturb its unmarred growth from post-war days –
And I was disturbed. Ivy was not for me as I needed no privacy
Coming as I did from a world where my life was an open book
With well-meaning interest on public trains – in my marriage,
    my income,
My family history and background, my opinions, my present
    identity.
I had not the wealth of family or nations, or dignity of title
To own and be guarded jealously by the familiarity of ensconcing
    ivy.

My Scottish home had not the grandeur of a manor house
Or the authenticity of an old English cottage to deserve my
    patronage.
I did have a makeshift tiled shed caressed by insidious ivy.
I could put back the grey tiles and replace them with rice thatch

If the climate was more benign. Then I could grow
Pumpkin and gourd, the poorer cousins of ivy. I could nurture
My neighbourhood and family with bountiful fruits of the
    tropics.
But that was not to be. In our absence,
When our West Coast friend, in a bid to demolish
The outmoded lean-to shed, cut back its protecting foliage
And without intention, uprooted the ivy where it began its
    journey
Under his axe, the branches buckled, the leaves shrivelled up.
I came back to see grey, wilting remnants hanging limply
In defeated despair – a death I had not desired or directed
But brought on by the relentless pace of a changing history.

The Wonder that was India

The drumbeats of War
Were silenced by the
Compassion Ashoka saw
In a moment of revelation
Of the horror of war
That wrought his transformation

Harshavardhan shed
His royal attire
To distribute with the weight
Of his body in gold
To his entire State
As he became the mendicant –
The penitent without desire.

In the courts of Jahangir
The British envoy witnessed
The wonder that was India
In the Akhbari darbar
The religious savants
Debated with ardour.

As kingdoms became
Princely States, lagaan
Taxed the unyielding land,
Devoid of the succour of rain
Impoverishing the landlord,
Starving the ryot in his domain

Into this land which fed
The factories elsewhere
Its men who obeyed orders
On other shores to shoot,

Quell and cower the other, thus
Becoming the hated arm of power.

Into this land which was told
It had no history, no culture,
No literature that could stand
The test of time, were born the stars
Of freedom, the valuers of the past
The dreamers of tomorrow.

They had diverse paths
To truth, spoke tongues
That emerged from the vastness
Of a home that had become
The glowing furnace of a
Smelting transformation

A protean reality
Of accommodation
Forged by a common
Aspiration to reclaim
Rejuvenate and revive
The wonder that was India.

Gokhale's prescient wisdom,
Patel's unflinching iron will
Chittaranjan's democratic embrace
Ambedker's epoch-changing skill
Sarojini's distinctive melody
Merged in a full throated appeal

That woke up a volcano
That was India, dormant
But not extinct, in an upsurge
Of action that marched

With Gandhi to the coast
To claim the salt in a fresh urge

To make history, to restore
Shakuntala and Meghdoot
As the paean to love and life
The simplicity of India's roots
Rich with the hope of revival
Brought by the cloud messenger

It was the age of ideology
Of invention and progress
Of Meghnad Saha, J.C. Bose,
Prafulla Chandra Roy and Satyen Bose –
Their dedicated minds.
The powerful pens

Of Mulk Raj Anand,
Of Prem Chand
Of Rabindranath
And Kazi Nazrul
Who dared to dream
And dared to transcend

Their tethered nation's
Apathy, to lift the plug
And let the lava flow
Down to the plains
In a molten river
Swift to slash and burn

In a jhoom cultivation
That submerged the present
Encouraged the sleeping
Subsoil to recover
And be ready for renewal

In a fresh endeavour
To illuminate the wonder of India.

The abstinence, the simplicity
The sacrifice, the dignity
That made India
Is the India of the caravans
Which have come through time
Augmenting and expanding the nation.

A grasping brood now
Makes sacrifice a travesty
As the people's chosen
Strive to get rich quick
The millions are shorn
The gatekeepers' conscience worn

The variegated nation
Denied of its colourful appeal
Is now being swathed in saffron
That was once glimpsed in the forest
Hermitage of meditation and calm
Far from the portals of power.

Let the forests speak again
Let the rivers surge with life
Let the India of many human waves
Rise up once more and thrive.
Let the wonder that was India
Reclaim her highest place and name.

Note: *The Wonder That Was India* is the title of the study of Indian
history and culture by the renowned historian A.L. Basham.

Indians don't kiss

One long sultry afternoon when the neighborhood lay still
And even the bulbuls had drooped into a dreamless stupor
Shelley's skylark seemed elusive as my mind wandered at will,
Slicing the noontide silence that encroached like a smothering
  creeper

I had to throw any pretence of study aside, assailed
As I was by that overpowering demon – boredom!
What could I do – I wondered. My lungs inhaled
The displaced air whirred into life at random

By whirring blades that punctuated my misplaced dreams.
My eyes swept my parents' study, and settled smugly
On the closed cabinet of their bookshelf of old albums
Which I decided to rummage through, a scattered family

Coming together in simple shades of black, grey and white
My mother's stylish bob as she sat musing on Shah Jahan's life
My father debonair in a white suit, my aunties with tight
Long plaits, my granny chopping fish on a crescent knife

While her loyal guard kept watch, her ginger cat
Who remained forever grey in those scraps of reminiscence.
And there was my grandfather, tall and jacketed
Against the Nepal Himalayas, and I knew their green abundance

In spite of their grand dark shadow that rolled incessantly
Behind him with authority, while my other granddad leaned
  against
His old Ford, the deep shade of his hospital veranda
  persistently
Calling his conscientious self to dash in on a graver quest.
And then, as I turned yet another page, I found a secret
Folded in the black pages of this still life history
– A green aerogramme from another era, in perfect

Folds, fragile but true, telling a forbidden love story

That I knew, but was not meant to read. But I did –
With trepidation and embarrassment, as tender words
Of undying love were pledged by my father, which he hid
So cautiously from his family, but were now poured

Without restraint to my mother from the distance
Of a workplace away from the city where she was.
And what shocked me then was the final instance
Of his attachment, sealed with not just love, but a kiss

In fact, with many kisses. I folded the letter away
As it singed my fingers with this burning sense
Of a new revelation. I was troubled and dismayed
For I had been led to believe that Indians don't kiss.

In my India

In the India that I knew
My mother met my father
In the portals of knowledge,
Debated freely while their
Coffee grew cold under the
Noisy fans of the Coffee House.

In my India my parents
Married across caste
Norms, accepted by both
Families – my mother for her
Grace and mellifluous voice
My father for his gentleness and brilliance.

In the India that I knew
I was valued as a girl
In my extended family
Who glowed at every dance drama
I choreographed and performed.

In my India my intrepid
Mother could rush out
Of her university classroom
To stop a vast crowd of students
From political campaigning in her domain

In the India that I knew
My father could confront
A police force intent on
Arresting Naxalites from
The Student Halls on the university campus.

In my India my Brahmin
Father, displaced by Partition
Could employ a Muslim cook
And my mother leave me in
The care of Amina's mother –
Our devoted matriarchs.

In the India that I knew
A girl molested on a bus
Would have the conductor
And driver and a whole
Angry crowd protecting her dignity.

In the India that I loved
I could cycle through a forest
Walk back alone as dawn
Broke after a sitar concert,
The Bhairav following my footsteps.

In the India where my youth
Blossomed, young men made
Witty remarks that made us blush
With pleasure as we walked past,
Basking in the admiration of their glance.

In my India we danced
At Holi, ate biryani at Eid
Watched a thousand lamps
Shine at Buddha Purnima, lit
Candles at Easter, and had a roast dinner
Watched by a resplendent Christmas tree.

In the India that I knew
We believed that education
Was a tool the caste-born and
Caste-less, the displaced and dispossessed

Could use to sharpen their reason and prosper.
In my India politics was about
A land reform movement,
About better distribution,
About social service, about destroying
Corruption by dreaming idealists.

In the India that I knew
No one told me what to wear,
What to practise, what to eat
Whom to marry, whom to claim
As my friend, companion, colleague and neighbour.

In my India we were moving
With the world, pushing orthodox
Boundaries, countering ignorance
In the Spirit of Rabindranath
In tune with Gandhiji's tolerance.

In my India we were modern
We nurtured the petals of culture
We were sustained by creativity
We revered our grandmothers
And mothers who had won our
Freedoms for us, opening India's door wide.

Give me back my India!

The Midnight Calls

When the fingers of the night curl around
One half of the reeling globe
Enwrapping supine souls in told dreams,
Some lie awake, having travelled
From the other part, physically here
While their thoughts dare jet miles
And enter the sun swathed world
Of those they left behind,
Reliving their every irksome chore,
Their compulsive duties, their age-weary moments,
While the would-be sleeper's reluctant ear is half alert
Fearing those midnight and small hour calls
'Hello... hello... yes, I can hear you
Can you hear me? Is everything all right
What... what has happened... when?'
Expectant, yet not welcoming the news,
Knowing each interruption, each intrusion
Is a message of another departure
As one more name is struck off
The phone book, not to be reached
Again in long distance voice links
Though remembered in a smile
And a sense of comfort
That will remain amidst a consciousness
Of a void, as part of a life that is not yet
Buried under an archaeological pile
Of forgotten histories.

The Meeting Point – Mohona
Here by a reflective river
Reminiscing on a boat-building past
The turquoise hull of *Buena Vista*
Stands still, its journeys over.
Here I am a heron taking flight
On a wing of fancy
Able to dream of a riverine terrain
And conjure a mohona
Of meetings the boats once intended.

Here where discarded columns
And supportive concrete arms
Hold back bridges and roads
Letting echoes swirl around
Of traffic above and footsteps below,
I am a swan in a quartet
Waddling with my tribe
Across the empty road
To the weaving river
To wade as dawn breaks,
Offering silent prayers
In ablutions I have seen
Performed by millions
In another *mohona*.

Here where cars sneak in
To stay parked away from
The magpie eye of traffic wardens,
I emerge – the urbanised seagull
Uncertainly approaching the motorised
Milieu, hoping to find a break
In the flow, to rush across the road
My wings forgotten,
The 'WAIT' button – an unlearnt language,
A flown-in customer

From a mohona,
Waiting to embrace this generous space
As the Pride of the Clyde glides by
Watched by the city and the migrant me.

Peter McCarey

Variations for Richard Peck

On Monday 9 June Mr Richard Peck, a specialist in
  diarrhoeal
diseases with the World Health Organisation
Jumped into the Ganges after a 10-year-old child who was in
  difficulty.
The body of Mr Peck was found on Friday, 35 miles
  downstream.
The body of the child has not yet been recovered.

Ah but it was a reckless thing to do:
The surface turns as slow as an old LP
But in there even a sinking stone
Will float like a tone-arm.

Roped up on a ridge of wind and gravity I asked
What if I slip? – You won't – All right, what if *you*
Slip? – If I fall off one side
You must jump off the other side at once.

According to Herodotus one King Cyrus of Assyria
Lost a favourite horse to the river as he marched on Babylon.
He exacted prompt revenge by having his army dig 180
  channels
on either side, to kill its force
Then he went on to take Babylon. God has done the same to
  poetry.

Heraclitus somewhere says that all things are in process and
nothing stays still
And likening existence to the stream of a river he says

That you would not jump twice
Into this same river.

As raindrops hit the navy-blue plastic cloth on the table outside
They send across the puddles little grey ball-bearings of water
That last as long as meteors,
Long as the surface tension holds.

Camus somewhere writes of a girl at the parapet of a bridge;
A man walks by and hears a splash as she jumps off.
At another point a man is standing on a bridge,
Startled by a disembodied laugh.
A great bag of water will form
On the leaf of a nasturtium
Then fall.
The leaf springs up like a branch when a pigeon has gorged
  itself
on plums and fluttered off.

A little bird skewers the Ganges with fire,
Hefts it up
And drowns it in the air.
A corpse gets bobbed under then burned on the ghats.

A jasmine
Garland sinking
After you in stinking
History.

Alexander the Great in the Hindu Kush
Played by Richard Burton ('No, not yet!')
A voice that howled for resonance in the Welsh hills
Dies out between the Jura and the Alps.

Ganges – you'd say the name of a Greek god,
But she's a mother goddess.
Negative theology:
Take leave of your mind and dive into the dark.

If the Bodhisattva knew all things (including the one who knows)
to be unreal,
The adjectival saviour of virtual beings from no danger,
This life no more than a juggle of statistics,
Why should he leave the cusp of an empty flood to rescue me?

Truth is sunk
In information,
Justice
In good offices.

The Ganges as a holy song above the mountain
Set out in a great scroll by the Gomukh glacier,
Expanded to several volumes in Varanasi,
With chemical and cloacal marginalia taking over.
The flux – the river as some unclean intestine
And the way to cope with it no wonder drug
But clean water, a little sugar and salt,
Patience and a kind word. You were the kind word.

The hiatus as the cord snakes out before you
The echo of a shout

No rainy Sunday afternoons left for you Mr Richard Peck
No memory no reflection.
You decided in one moment who you are; you staked your life
on it
And won.

From the Sanskrit

'We give an example of an *ekaksara* stanza, employing
only one consonant throughout:
Dadado dudda-dud-dadi
dadado duda-di-da-doh
dud-dadam dadade dudde
dad'-adada-dado 'da.dah'

Did I do Dido? Wd I dodo
DD? Do IOU a dead id?
D-day, de-wedded, I did dhow.
'Aid Dido, dude,' ode daddy added,
'Aideed'd aid Aida'.
Da?
You'd owe a dewy-eyed ode, ide-oid.
Adieu. A dowdy odd doe O-D'd.

Artou/ Off the Map

In the map shop the music playing
was John Coltrane so far away
So far away, some rag-top Rolls
of a raindance raga, Indian English plosives
in the tabla's Vedic commentary.

The map I took to be Tamil Nadu
explained itself as Hindu Kush
(as fingerprinted by the Swiss).
As I looked down, to touch the names
in the folds of Kashmir beaten in lines

by nimble hooves and bangled heels,
Srinagar joined Schiehallion
(the first hill caught in contours), Lochnagar
and every trait I'd flatten out, beyond my span
of days for sensing the ribcage rise, a country's cadences.

Due to this earthquake hit

Due to this earthquake hit lakhs of people
had been lost their family member their shelter,
they are in very drugedy condition.
Most of the people have lost their hands, legs eyes,
and were hardly injured. This seems to us very sad
and undiagestable.

We write this letter with tears of lakhs of people
this quake hit really affected 5 Districts.
In these affected area
6 villages are our service area in this six village
95% of the buildings and thacted roofs and were fully destroyed
and they lost their all materials,
these affected people were needy of MEDICAL FIRST AID,
food and shelter, at least temporary huts,
clothes, foods, medical treatments. Many families have lost
their heads (Husband or wife) many children lost both
their father and mother, we also write this letter with tears.

Note: This found poem comes from a letter received by
the United Nations 1% for Development Fund.

From the Metaforest

Brahman denotes the term to be defined
and âtman that which defines it;
by Brahman the limitation implied in âtman is removed,
and by âtman the conception of Brahman as
a divinity to be worshipped is condemned.

I have studied, most reverend sir,
the Rigveda, Yajurveda, Sâmaveda,
the Atharvaveda as fourth, the epic
and mythological poems as fifth veda,
grammar, necrology, arithmetic, divination,
chronology, dialectics, politics, theology,
the doctrine of prayer, necromancy, the art
of war, astronomy, snake-charming and the fine arts, –
these things, most reverend sir, have I studied;
therefore am I, most reverend sir,
learned indeed in the scripture,
but not learned in the âtman.
Yet I have heard from such as are like you
that he who knows the âtman vanquishes sorrow.
I, however, most reverend sir, am bewildered.
Lead me then over, I pray,
to the farther shore that lies beyond sorrow.

Note: 'From the Metaforest' is drawn from Paul Deussen,
The Philosophy of the Upanishads, translated by A.S. Geden, 1906,
reprinted New York, Dover, 1966.

Adolesce

As we got to the first floor landing I asked you out.
You smiled and said no, you had to meet your cousin.
I was glad you had a cousin. I was glad grey light
had moored the banister.
Tenements were sandstone, that I knew,
but I wondered what stone the steps were –
grey as light, worn as driftwood beams,
as lips or shinbones I could have kissed,
like the lintel of a shore temple,
caressed and corroded by winds and visitors.

Eclampsia. Give me some light!
The body brown and bulbous, eclipse

Of the tallow sun in the clean mud room.
Cramp, and the eyes are at maximum aperture

It's a trench, this, a camp on the Somme:
Bulls-eye for the ordnance of corporate

Crapatopia. Last time, the husband cap in hand
And the baby fished out like a carp from a pond.

This time – has he left her a dose of the clap
Before eating the pesticide he couldn't pay for?

Clasp at the dark, lady,
A last twist of silver that held up your hair –

Your molars still clamp as the next one
Takes your breast.

4-6-12

Buy your Bombay mix with rupees
From the Mumbai mint.

Beware of those moustachioed
Greek demigods from Gandahar,

But script their myths of solitude
For Bollywood. Don't miss a trick, so

Little Miss Minx can mince in her minks
A Bangalore rhythm in workaday pinks,

Rings on her mitts, polo mints on her toes,
Steak mince and tatties wherever she goes.

9.2.12

A wren on the branch above his head
In the mango orchard round an ancient stupa.
This is bliss! He tokes his pipe.
He didn't know the Indians had wrens.
But they didn't know that Cornishmen had sharks.
Rehearsing the honoured tropes with which it's done
He toasts absent friends. That takes a while.
A servant totes the tiffin hamper back to barracks.

Alan Riach

Passages from India: Three Poems

I never can make out what it is. Sacrifice, fate, perhaps death
itself; something that is always close, everywhere. I suppose it is
death, of which there is so much. But there is an exhilaration in
it, I don't know why.
> Violet Jacob, *Diaries* (1897)

I know some twenty capitals. Bah!
> *But then there is Calcutta.*
>> Henri Michaux, *A Barbarian in Asia* (1945)

I: Calcutta

My father has been here before.
It is a dream. What happens to you later
cannot be predicted. Kiddapore Docks.
The sky is full of the bridge, this fretworked grid of steel,
and all its weight is clamped across the city.
Its 27,000 tons bear down, and yet
the life below is far from being crushed: it crushes,
crashes round itself, its market is unending.

Washing, getting filthy, drinking, eating,
passing it all, the fires in the dusk in the alleys
and streets, the orange light in the dun living twilight.
Thin men leaning on a wall or bench or car
bonnet, fat men in the restaurants, women
walking quietly, their eyes alert and looking.

It is as if the men are watching, the women,
different, looking. Unobtrusively. The children have not
settled, yet, just how to use their eyes.
They are full of surprise, and active.

My father has been here before me.
At the start of the world and after the end of the war,
the Merchant Navy Clanline brought him in,
standing on the bridge, a young man, First Mate,
leaning into the world for the first time then.

Brown smoke from the traffic,
the permanent grit in the air, in your hair,
the sticky asphalt of the road,
the broad drifts of dust,
the refuse risen in contours,
hardened into the earth itself,
and the salvaging, the raking through
the residue for sustenance –
what power might be derived
from broken things.

Ubiquitous as dust,
intimate in nostrils and lungs,
felt in the eyes and tasted in the mouth,
it is about the place, a sense
of what we owe ourselves,
a debt unpaid, an uncrossed cheque,
a state of how becoming
may be coming clearer.
What cruelty, distressful, is the fact,
yet there is this presence here,
this marvellous disturbance.

Beyond the rage and bloodshed, as there is,
is also this persistence:
the mutiny of the tyrannised,
the fact of validation.

What world is this, to hold us all?
What happens to you later
cannot be predicted. But it is not a dream.
These lives are real, the river, bridge, the people,
the commerce and the currents take us all.

II: Remembrance

'The biggest thing that hit me I remember. I was eighteen years old.
We sailed into Cochin on the Malabar coast, with an Indian crew,
to change the crew. It was 1948. We'd to pay them all off,
and get a new crew. It was a Clanline ship, the *Clan MacAuley*.
We were carrying wool from Australia, bound for Liverpool and
    Glasgow.
I was a cadet. (My earliest voyage, the first voyage I did
was all apples: 192,000 cases of apples, from Tasmania,
bound for Liverpool, and Glasgow. That was maybe, 1947.)

'But it was India that hit me. It hit me like the biggest wave I ever
    saw,
higher than a house, that swept away the lifeboats, and I was on
    the bridge,
looking out. That was how India hit me: poverty, the way the
    people
did what they did, on shore, like nothing I had ever seen,
eighteen years old, from Stornoway on Lewis and from Mull and
    Dingwall.
Nothing I had ever seen was like that. That's how I remember it.'

III: Kolkata

Howrah Bridge –
     moving, seen through traffic
between buildings, above people –
people on the pavements and crossing the roads, in crowds
and crowds, people in the buildings,
passing through doorways, entering, leaving,
every building now this taxi drives me past, and above,
in the windows, moving, and above the buildings, the bridge,
moving, and beyond the traffic, buses, people, packed with
 people,
and inches from the taxi window, the sides of buses, scarred
 and dented,
moving in the constant noise of horns and shouting, talking,
 moving,
rising over the people and the traffic and the buildings,
the bridge rising into the dust and mist and brown and grey
polluted air come down to rest on its highest structures, they
rising into it, it meeting them, folding into them,
inhumanly high and intimate,
Howrah Bridge –
     So the taxi takes me through the streets
and the maze of routes, the labyrinth,
these canyons of Kolkata,
till we come to the great whirlpool,
the gulf of the circular roads around
the central railway station. And now the bridge is close,
looming. The traffic stops at the lights and all
the engines are switched off
as the crowds pour off the pavements, over the roads,
to the other sides, torrential surge of movement,
sensitized as people are, but caught among and moving along
these huge, irreversible tides.
     And now to cross,
the bridge takes us on and into its structure.

The current drives us all along its span.
For a minute or two or three, perhaps,
the vast tranquil shape of the river below
is seen in the twilight of pink, ochre, delicate
grey, and I roll the window down
as the January air rolls in, cool and
suddenly clean, and the ships along the river
can be seen in their separate places,
moving or at anchor in the commerce
of their cargoes and the purpose
of their destinations. –
     And then it's over, we're over,
and the curve round the road takes us back,
to return, crossing once again,
back through the city, back to
where we came from.
     Howrah Bridge behind us
and the river far below.

The Temples of Bishnupur

Baked earth temples, where the fired body is porous.
How does this work? Monsoon rains drench all,
But there they are, that should have melted wet in the wash
And drained and dribbled away, solidified like candle wax,
But they stand in their various stalwart clay red forms,
Each one a sculpture, arcs and arched doorways, outer walls
Of small framed panels, depicting: Ganesh, Siva, Varuna, men
And women, carriages and animals, cows and collocations
Of the visible world, elephants engaged in the act of coition,
Mounted, each panel an astonishment, hundreds of them,
On each side wall. One temple's roof's a pyramidal lift
Of straight diagonal lines, converging; another's is as swift
A symmetrical curve as a scimitar's blade, four curves,
Balanced; another's uses square shapes; all are brazen,
Terra cotta red, and smell of cold earth. The air is wet and warm.
My guides and I walk round and enter them, slowly, one
After another, until enough's enough. My head bowed
For the low arch, entering, I hear a voice, 'Be careful
For the snakes.' I've seen the birds and bats. 'The snakes?'
'These temples are old. Their shadows are cool. There are
Snakes, sometimes. Be careful.' Gods bless the observant,
Those who take care and precaution. And time. Thunder rolls.
We take our bodies back to the car, our porous thoughts
Holding what we can, keeping things in balance and
   momentum, slow.

Entering India

It's tumbling into the world –
Dream of a fall, mind
A leap, an arabesque that opens limbs then
Closes in the air like scissors then curls all limbs into
A world of torso, falling in a thickly cushioned air,
Warm and wet and wombtime, softening,
Comforting, as the whole body rolls,
Within this, descending, yet buoyant, while the earth
Is there below, not to be feared, your arms again extend
As your mind extends, to touch,
To make connections, to start the friction slowly
That will slow the impact down, but
No impact comes, simply a settlement into
A context, a world you did not know was there,
You might be in, where all the
Coloured tracks and trails and elephant roads
And territories mapped and bordered
Are not as they were, not as you had known,
Without former reference, only
This touching, this movement,
This saying hello in the human
Universe, hopefully, empty hands extended –

Gerry Singh

India Gate

The noon sun over Delhi
Lit up the M8.

On my soft shoulder
Was a hard shoulder
Laying out a long carpet
To the pink city of Jaipur.

Looking towards the Lomonds
I saw a lama
On the cooling heights of Shimla
Walking on a cloud of dust.

And a small train
Rattling the iron gauges
Fuelling a trip to the Ganges.

Waiting on the platform
At Varanasi
I met so many strangers
Who had been here before.

Watched them
Bathing in the warm light
Where Emperors had stood
Not hearing the thundering clatter
Of the Raj.

And reflected in the churned
Up waters of the flood
Was a lovely child of both.

Frances Ainslie

The Paisley Frock

Ah mind thon frock,
sae soft against ma skin.
A tear-drop pattern it was.
Teal-blue and broon
wi' tortoiseshell buttons.
I can still hear ma mither's voice –
Haud still till I pin yer hem.
See how bonnie it hangs?
Gie us a twirl.

She stitches and spins tales
aboot silks fae Kashmir
carried o'er fog-tangled oceans.
Skeins, laid in wooden kists
wi' spices, tea and indigo.
Silks, that Paisley wifies weave
intae cloth that she sews.
Her gift,
for a daft besom like me.

Plant Hunting

A low thrum rouses me
 fae summer sleep.
There, cupped in a poppy,
the bumbees hairy knees
skirl and strain.
It keeks oot,
its towsy pow dusted
wi' golden plunder.
Swag-laden, it flies
starboard home.
Meconopsis Himalaya
nods her heid and
trims back her blue sails.
Her blousy petals
fade in the afterglow.

Rain

Today I hoped for sunshine,
yet, the rain came
in squalls
that scudded across
the minch fae Skye.
Dreich it was, tho' nothin
like that night in Mumbai
when shards of light
slashed open
a beetle-black sky.

Street dogs slunk in pairs,
two by two, gulpin' like fish.
Rickshaws drowned
on the river highway.
Drookit as rats in a burn,
bairns splashed in the streets
knee-deep in smiles as
the days despair
slithered out on the tide.

One more day of hope-
hope that lives only in rain.

Northern Lights

I wait for the northern sky to change –
for a shift of light.
I forget to breathe
as Aurora shimmers in.
An interference of ultramarine,
violet and emerald green.
A tail-fan of peacock feathers
with quills of carnelian red that
paint henna-tattoos across the sky.
Light-headed, I teeter
on the rim of a new world,
till all that remains
is the smell of rain
and the sky.

Bombay

From the sea-wall, strands of light
thread west to Malabar Hill.

A pearl necklace, you say –
 candled by the moon.

A different sky strung with
pearls and splintered stars.

Will I ever be as precious
as this city that you love?

The Bombay night
seems lost for words.

Across the world, Scotia's river Tay
flows molten with silver light.

It calls me home.
Still, I leave behind

a tiny seed of sand
caught in your mantle.

Streets

Outside Waverley station,
dawn mist obscures the
molehill humps of blanket
that stud the grey pavement
upwards to the old town.
Yet, I think of her,
the girl in the yellow sari,
slinking cat-like between
cars in viscous smog.
The slow shuffle of flip-flops
on dusty, brown feet, as she
runs her finger down the glass.
I wonder where she is today, and if
she wears the tartan ribbon in her hair?

Rab Wilson

In Praise o Eternal Peace
*Owerset frae Sarojini Naidu (1879-1949), Indian political
activist, feminist and writer. The first Indian woman to be
president of the Indian National Congress.*

Men say the warld is fou o fear an hate,
An aa life's ripenin fields o hairst await
The fykie Rob Sorby o thrawn stour fate.

But Ah, sweet Sowl, gie thenks that Ah wis born,
When frae the fouthie meedows fou o corn
Ah watcht the gowden sangbirds o yer morn.

Whit care Ah fir the warld's desire an pride,
Wha ken the siller wings that glisk an glide,
Thae Doo's that hamewarts flee at eventide.

Whit care Ah fir the warld's lood weariness,
Wha dwams in gloamin's barns that you hae blesst
Wi wallie stooks o maumie seelences?

Else, wull Ah heed the dowie weird o doom,
Or dreid the clash o laneliness an gloom,
The dumb an eldritch grue gien bi the tomb?

Ma gledsome hairt is drunk an drencht wi ye,
O inmaist wun o leevin ecstacy!
O saicret souch, virr o eternity!

The Gowden Boat
Owerset frae Rabindrath Tagore (1861–1941)

Cloods rumblin i the lift; blaudin shooers.
Ah coorie-doun bi the riverside, dowf an alane.
The stooks lig gaithert,   hairst is ower,
The watter in spate gey near burstin its banks.
As we sheared the paddy it stairtit tae rain.

Ane wee paddy-field, nane but masel –
Flude-watters swirlin an pirlin aawhaurs.
Trees oan the faur side   slaister sheddaes lik ink
Oan a toun pentit grey in the mornin's daw.
Oan this side a paddy-field, wi nane but masel.

Wha is this, steerin inby the shore,
Singin? She haes the souch o a body ah ken.
The sails are happit wide,   she glowers aheid,
Waves brak tentlessly agin the boat aither side.
Ah luik an jalouse ah hae seen her face afore.

Oh tae whit fremmit launds dae ye sail?
Come tae the bank an tie-up yer boat fir a wee.
Gang whaur ye ettle,   gie care whaur ye may,
But cam tae the bank a meenit, an lowse yer smile.
Tak awa ma gowden paddy whan ye sail.

Tak it, tak as muckle as ye can cairry.
Hae ye mair? Naw, nane, ah hae stowed ye fou.
Ma eident darg   here bi the watter –
Ah hae pairtit wi it aa, the hale jing-bang:
Nou tak me as weel, be hamelie, tak me abuird.

Nae room, nae room, the boat is ower wee.
Ladent wi gowden paddy, the boat is fou.
Athort the drumlie lift   cloods heeze back an forrit,
Oan the bare-as-birkie bank, Ah bide alane –
Aa that ah had haes gane: the gowden boat taen aa.

Ah wis Deid, syne Leevin
Owerset frae Jalal ad-Din Muhammad Rumi (1207–1273)

Ah wis deid, syne leevin.
Greetin, syne lauchin.

The pooer o luve cam intil me,
an ah becam fierce lik a lion,
syne gentyl lik the starn o e'en.

He said, 'Ye're no gyte enow.
Ye dinnae belang this hoose.'

Ah went wud, wis boond haund an fuit.
He said, 'Aye-an-oan no wud enow
tae bide wi us!'

Ah bruck throu til anither level
intil joyfuness.

He said, 'It's no enow.'
Ah dee'd.

He said, 'Ye are a clevir wee chiel,
fou o ferlies an douts.'

Ah poukit oot ma feathers an becam a fuil.
He said, 'Nou ye are the cannle
fir this assemblie.'

But ah'm nae cannle. Luik!
Ah am jist airtless reek.

He said, 'Ye are Chief amang us, wir guide an maister.'
But ah'm nae dominie. Ah hae nae pooer.

He said, 'Ye aareadies hae wings.
Ah cannae gie ye wings.'

But ah hud a lang ee fir his wings.
Ah felt lik an auld hen, anchort tae the grund.

Then brent oangauns soucht i' ma lug,
'Dinnae muive. A byordnar gyft is
ettlin taewart ye.'

An auld luve whuspert, 'Bide wi me.'

Ah said, 'Ah wull.'

Ye are the well-heid o the sun's licht.
Whilst ah am the willow wand's sheddae oan the yird.
Ye turn ma tattertmallions tae buskit braws.

The saul at daw is lyk til daurkent watter
whaes mou slaely forms tae say Thenk ye, thenk ye.

Syne at close o day, agane, Venus tentie
chainges intil the mune syne til the hale lift o nicht.

This cams o smilin back
at your smile.

The Graundmaister hauds his wheesht,
ither than muivin his seelent pieces athort the buird.

That ah am pairt o the ploys
o this gemm maks me
unco happy.

Suhayl Saadi

Jacob's Seventh Dream

Deep in English earth
A silver locket bound in iron
Tooth, dirk, epistle
Azrael clasp

I, Jacobus filius Jacobi, King of Flodden Field, do repent of
all my sins
Save one
To Dunbar, to the Great Michael, to the Margarets both
The lands of my realm
The peoples, dead, living and yet unfleshed
And to my poor infant son
I rise through eternal parchment
As through another's life
And dream in tryptich:

I

The Black Book of Truth: words
Whispers gilded with skin
Hover through the wax darkness of woad ceremonies

The Ancient Club
Hortus Medicus Edinburgensis
Seekers of shorelines, hermeneutic founts and metrical
mountains

Matter pure, flesh distilled
From Pergammos, Cordoba, Louvain

And Long Ned, shusy-lifter
Cartographer of human form and flood
The Great Divider
Alpha and Omega, Aleph and Yae

II

Border crags sharpen
Shepherdess sleeps still
Winter moon turns granite earth
Crows judder sky

Blind Robber Black,
Darkens the grave face

Snake-head petals plucked
Tossed into blood bowl
The Surgeon-apothecary is Master again

Mort safe lock
Pig iron key
Cold night kiss,
Death cloth dance

Sunlight cracks ice
Fleam scarifications
Eyes dart thumb boned,
Bottle-jars and grease

Deacon barber-surgeon wrestles
Quaich whitened fingers across
Cadaver lover – shoulders, heart, swollen stomach –
Quill, palimpsest

The Seal of Cause:
Words, a murderer's bed
Up! The blade flares, then
Night

III

The Misses Nelly to the Burgess surgeon!
This very might, a performance
Of dissection – flexing leg, belly, supple loin and eye – each
one
Separated, given name, place
Her husk, raised from the cold necropolis
By the hand of a lover ghoul,
Taut, a bridge of tetany, nude again
Beneath the proscenium of bone

Ah, Nelly, Nelly!
Thy sweet scent hovers in the attic laboratory
The perfect geometer of thy span
Gleams like a moon
Thine hand, woven now in a darkening web
Once caressed another's cheek
And played the spinet
In a drawing-room gone into light and dust

Gentlemen! The first cut will be made by the Kirk-Maister!
Voltaic pile, chirurgery on a speck, gas dreams,
Spine arches, bone-upon-bone
Fists bunch and quiver as though to embrace a fire
Eyelids spring open, a terrified ecstasy
She lives again!
Now, Master Barber, now
Commence your thrift
In flashes of light and song

And spring-loaded blades –
But will Nelly reveal her secrets?

Poised thus above the oak table
I remember! These feet, lips, fingers once
ran on rough loch ground
winced a little, in breath,
tapped out chords of the spirit
Dust symphonies, numinous flesh
Together, through the skins of our lives
We laughed at death

In the grog-shop, the Great Doctor Liston
Can amputate a limb in thirty-three seconds!
One, two, three...
Gone, her left leg
Four, five, six...
Away, her right arm
Seven, eight, nine...
Her torso, hung like wet paper on a spit

If the brain-pan of Blind Ned Black were prised open
Would it reveal a great emptiness?

These hazel eyes,
Bathed in alchemical glass
A frisson of darkness in space
Love is not eternity

I wander in the night
Down lost alleyways
Past the ruined chapel
Where the bodies, newly-hung
I fancy, scream in the wind:
Guilty Ned, thy time is nigh!

Behind me, in serried ranks,
The clowns of the Anatomy Hall
Grin
The necks of lovers, pinned, swung, articulated in cases of
wood and glass
Rocked and swooned in noddies over the wild road
Sped through the moonless quantabulum

A pretence of priesthood
Black robes, watchers of the dead
From secret vaults 'neath the chirugion's hearth
The stench of whisky billows

At last, I have found her! Nelly, Margaret, Scotia
Wanders, lost, in the surgeon's physic garden
Leans with a sigh against Flodden wall
Twirls between phalanges the stem of a thistle
And dreams...

I reach out my white hand
Ah, my love!
Beneath the thinned voile, thine hair is finer, thy skin colder
than I remember
When last I slipped the cleik around thine ankle, laid
The pitch softly 'pon thy lips

Paradise Gardens Carpet
(for the National Museums of Scotland, 2002)

Glasgow: Mantle of the Green Hollow

One morning,
by the exquisite scent of sweet alyssum we were drawn
from the wild peacock reeds of the cold green river
to the centre of the City of the West Wind
to a caravanserai in a wall with no gate

From behind the Wall of Thenew came the ragim creaks of
  water-wheels
through its cracked substance fired shafts of white light
we, the shadow people of the borders,
each from another place
peered through many fissures,
separate niches, each
saw a different garden beyond the wall,
discussed, at length decided we
the gardens must be infinite

The garden was a robe with eight sides, many levels
the sky, a dome of blue and white flowers
petals, fluttering, changing in form
rolling into one another like cloud-banks
each bagh was four, seamed by
rivers of wine, honey, water, milk
flowing through the palms of water-wheels,
quadrants dividing again and again
into yet smaller squares, each
filled with the floating forms of cypresses ringed by citrus groves:
lime, orange, lemon
lime trees formed hijaabs, shading the fragile from the light,
while pungent lemon kept away stray vermin and

mihrab orange trees led to garden rooms and plaster courts
where on eight-sided tables, antique scrolls
wrote upon themselves in Kufic script with reed quills
and seeds burst joyously from the skins of pomegranates

Stone pavilions striped in ochre, black and terracotta
sheltered beneath mulberry trees, rock and leaf shadows,
reflected in the uisge of tiny lochs,
danced in the House of Joy that was the garden
scent of Damask roses, heavy
of musk sweat, camphor wood and ginger plant, we smelled
and the white baadil of jasmine turned us
into night-dancers and weeping willows and laughing children

And as we were spun into beggars, falcons and pigeons,
so were the letters on the scrolls changed
into gazelles and lions, dragons and phoenixes
and at length there was no longer any sun and moon
but only the sides of a tambourine, dancing and swaying,
bells tinkling like the sound of water through stone
And all the music of the jannat:
the birdsong, the water, the emptiness
came to one, single note: Peace

At the centre of the chahar bagh, into which all streams
 flowed,
lay a basin built on the backs of twelve stone bulls
and from the basin came, not water merely, but
a giant, tortuous vine with branches bowing far into the sky
meandering foliage, ladders and wings, leaves split
by wondrous caterpillars weaving shimmering silken veils

As we shaded our eyes from the blinding noor,
we saw above the trees a gate, the shape of re-joined badams,
beyond this, a trellis bearing tiny blossoms around a giant,
 eight-petalled flower

four gates barring different layers of the garden
each bearing the petals of different flowers:
snowdrops, tulips, roses and gentian trumpets
On the lower branches of the vine tree, perched
two calligraphic birds and a silver fish, all gazing into
a spherical hanging glass in which burned a lamp

When we returned to our homes, everything had changed
The river, once-glaucous, flowed down from the mountains
  like liquid diamond,
the city had turned from frozen tomb to burning bedchamber,
rhythms of reel and iron flowed as blood through our veins
that which had enclosed the courtyard of our bodies was no
  longer
we were free, yet we were blind

In the centre of each house, a tall loom
across the floor, threads of many shades
we were blind yet
like worm, seed-hair and lustrous pashm,
we knew by touch and smell and taste the colour of every thread

We set to work, each on a different carpet, a separate loom
we strove to reproduce what we had seen
but wool, cotton and silk are not petals and streams and stars
our hands, human not divine, so
the beings emerging from the taut weft and weave
had not life, breath, words, but were merely simulacra
as music is to the whisper of the Friend's breath

We were stone blind, had no pattern,
only our memories, and the memories of those who had gone
  before
for this work spanned many generations, the pain of countless
  partings,
it moved with us

across darya, desert, moss and law
We wove herbaceous borders of irises, lilies and bluebells
planted polygons of tulips, hyacinths, guls
beneath the tips of our fingers, palm fronds became
vine leaves and lotus blossoms
fissures and tolls in stone opened
into window-frames and ladders and the kairi of ancient
  mango trees
the dun splendours of the city which we could never have had,
strutted and moaned as peacocks
ancient scrolls, which we could never have read,
we wrote as filigree silver and gold
dark places, into which by a thousand armies we were cast,
we fashioned as wild asses,
wings upon which we were denied flight,
we grew as almonds
Beinn Kaaf, up whose steep, horn sides we clambered,
the skin of our hands tearing from the bone,
we dreamed as a black pyramid
The Loved One, as a gazelle.

When the slowest carpet was finished,
the last trump fashioned,
the final hole cut in the shehnai reed of the unseen farishta,
we found that we did not know how to tie the end knot
left in that state, the carpets soon would unravel, their paths,
become lost in the furze and brash and musk of the green hollow
so we hauled the rugs into the courtyard by the unknown river
upon our hunched shoulders one, great loom
and using this frame, with our fingertips we sewed the ends of
each carpet to the beginnings of another,
so that the whole became one, great carpet with neither
beginning nor end

And then we moved our homes to the rug,
and sat and lived and swam upon it as upon dark water,

and like the words on the scrolls in the pavilions,
it grew within us, and so
we began the weaving of an endless carpet, one
which can be added to by every guest who passes through our
  homes,
each traveller may leave their mark,
their vision of the gardens, become heart,
upon the green earth of our place
until eventually
the carpet will spread out and cover
the mountains, the lochs, the world
Our pain is turned to laughter, our blindness to light

Edinburgh: The Calligraphies of the Mirror

By the light of the windy, rising sun, we sailed up the slow-
  moving fjjordr
and came upon the face of a hill and a cluster of houses
Disembarking, with our laughing children, we let loose our
  ships and watched
as they vanished like swords over the horizon into the burning
  fire of the east

But the town, old and new, was deserted, the flanks of its
  buildings,
cold stone mute
carrying only our bones and the threads of our sinews,
we tramped over muir and burn and through raivels of dying
  reeds
until we came to the medina of the city,
drawn in the form of a rectangle open to the sky
and there, young and old Mothers of the Voyage, we sat down
The wind swooped from the north-east like a giant albatross

our limbs grew cold and blue, our faces, turned toward the
  face of the hill,
moved slowly upon the granite earth
we heard only shadow music, for we were the Mothers of the
  Vanished,
we had lost everything

Then the sun rose to the nuun point,
into the dark blue sky shadows fled
we rose from the ground and with our bones for tools,
we hewed rock from the buildings, pink and grey,
from the cold walls of the community centres,
and we mounted these stones into an arch

And from this mihrab, from this centre, in strict and perfect
  geometer,
we began to spin the silken threads of our sinews into rivers,
trees, flowers
as we worked, day and night and day, we talked and danced
  and sang,
our laughing scissors cut templates of a new aesthetic,
raised tufts of a thousand layers
drew sentences rising and falling and changing
like the waves of the northern sea from whence we had come

At the heart of our ferdaus was a great tree, from which
in threads of silver and gold wound around silk like runs of
  notes around a stave,
there flowed four rivers
at its end, each river sank into four mihrabs
and along the length of each stream
fluttered butterflies with wings of many different colours

With bloodied hands, we drew reeds from the earth
spun the flax from their heads into maqam patterns
which repeated,

one layer upon the next,
to a hundred, a thousand,
to the unknowable,
differing each by only the breadth of a butterfly's wing

In this way, we carved our paridaeza into the air and stone of
  the fjjodr city,
each petal, one deed, transfigured
a northern forest of columns, of pine and spruce and falcon nests,
of clearings along the way where
blooded roses and piteous carnation beggars prostrate
  themselves,
of earth tachts above sunken streams
where the dark, scented bells of hyacinths ring and weep, aiai!,
and where tulips martyr their slender necks,
not for monotonous uniformity or the empty, lying graves of war
but for harmonious balance, for symmetry of word, mind, action,
for the unity of ishq and liberty
Breath, peace

Hands henna'd with soil,
we began at the centre-point and wove outward in harmonic
  geometer,
the forms of fish, insects, sea eyes
and as we wove beneath the cold moon, we heard,
coming from the upper branches of our tree,
the sound of unseen, bagpipe'd farishtas
playing the dialectical songs of our voyage, of our progress,
writing our names in the weave in a script which could be read
only by dying nightingales

From the garden pavilions of palaces to the earth mohallas of
  beggars,
from the Court of the Archives to the golden drawing-rooms
  of the saints,
we carved cedar columns, tile mosaics and moulded stucco,

grew dates and pomegranates,
cut inscriptions in steel globes
in the shapes of spiralling vines and birds of light

Along vertical levels, we raised transparent curtains of water,
through which, at certain times of day,
it was possible to see the shapes of distant cypresses
hijaabs of the soul; freedom of the mind and body
At the four points, we opened seven gateways, weft and weave,
each one deeper than the next,
and amidst summer meadows of violets,
beneath each we planted a treasury of secrets

And at the centre of the forest, was a pool covered with water
  lilies
into which everything flowed
and in whose depths, everything changed
in the surface of the water, a walnut tree, a spherical yew,
on an island in the middle of the lake
approached by four, vine-draped pergolas
a square pavilion with eight-sided minarets of white marble
roved by jasmine and mallow and myrtle,
with heavy, cedarwood doors guarded by stone turtles and
  singing amphorae,
the pavilion was the tomb of the lost symmetries,
through its black, foursquare, wrought-iron windows
shone a great white light, flowed
rivers of silk, blown on a pine wind
out through the forest to the lanterns and towers of the city
  beyond
up into the sky, to the diamond stars

At last, we were finished,
we stood back, admired our work
in our garden, our carpet, we had gathered together

the True, the Good and the Beautiful, through these
we sought the idea, drew
the world into our arms, turned it
into a book

To feel one's feet upon the carpet,
to stride through the garden among the silent, singing
Friends,
is to walk through the poems of that book
better still, to bend down beneath the shadows of scholartrees
to grab from the stream a cup of wine, to drink,
to compose a poem in the flower mirror

Yet still, it remains a transient, shimmering residence
of fragrant islets and water pergolas,
of cloud walls and pomegranate windows...

This is just the beginning, the first station,
to become that bird which is so free
it can carry the tiniest petal out into the limitless universe
can be the work only of the One

Paradise Garden Party Glossary

Most of the words are from Farsi or Urdu, except where otherwise indicated.

aiai: hyacinth (Greek)
baadil: clouds
badam: almond
bagh: garden
Beinn: Mount (Scots Gaelic)
caravanserai: resting-place for caravans
chahar: four
darya: river
farishta: angel
ferdaus: Paradise/garden (Farsi/Urdu)
fjjordr: firth, an long inlet of the sea (Old Norse)
guls: roses
henna: brownish dye for hair or skin
hijaabs: veils; head-coverings
ishq: spiritual love
jannat: garden; Paradise (Arabic)
kairi:seeds (of the mango)
Kaaf: letter of Arabic alphabet symbolising The Clear Book, sublime truth, the Word, the hidden treasure, alchemical changes; also a mythical mountain on the path of enlightenment
Kufic: angular form of Arabic script, long obsolete in manuscripts/ books, but still used on architecture
maqam: unit in Arabic music; basic style of a piece
mihrab: prayer niche in the wall of (especially) a mosque
muir: moor (Scots)
mohallas: alleyways
nuun: letter of Arabic alphabet, signifying prophecy, nobility, breath; concise knowledge in the presence of Oneness
noor: light
Paridaeza: Paradise (Old Farsi)
pashm: soft, smooth underfur (e.g. in cashmere); wool
ragim: as pertaining to a raag, a unit of North Indian music
raivels: tangles (Scots)
shehnai: flute

tachts: thrones
Thenew: St Thenew was the mother of St. Kentigern/Mungo, the
patron saint of Glasgow
tolls: holes (Scots)
uisge: water (Scots Gaelic)
wahdat: spiritual unity (Arabic)

Jameela Muneer

The Scottish Way

Full school uniform she wore,
maroon blazer, tartan skirt
black tights, tie and SOMETHING more.
'Hijab' her reply was curt.
9/11 rocked the world –
daughter mine, found religion
when violent abuse was hurled
and latent racism unfurled.
Strictly her own decision.
Shabina Begum unleashed?
No. While we did not agree,
knew, we must support her 'Free
Will' – let her dress as she pleased –
A matter of self-belief.
Anxious wait for the phone calls,
angry missives from school,
strained 'chats' in Guidance halls
about discipline and 'the rules'
But – NOTHING! She was ignored.
No one made a fuss, floored
she stopped of her own accord.
We heaved a sigh of relief
Life carried on as before.

Stockbridge Man

The right background,
Scottish by birth.
A Cambridge man,
I know my worth

Fortune favours me.
At this I rejoice.
Live in a basement
entirely by choice

I need no help
I can stand alone.
'Struth, believe me, a
Sylvester Stallone.

I know this town
like the back of my hand
Played all the venues
I know where I stand.

There is no subject
on which I cannot discourse
I know everything
about women of course.

A man in my position
can look where he pleases.
No time for Buddha
Moses, or Jesus.

Fastidious in taste,
My vices are few.
All I desire is
a girl with a view.

I'm a gentleman too.
You may be misled.
I shan't correct you –
just the texts you have read

1993

Comprehensive Eid 2015

Eid Prayers done, and debts to pay:
English should be my remit –yet
'Our Modern Language Sir's away:
Could we get her for French today?"'
What reason to object? See me
Speaking pure Urdu fluently
In Edinburgh Catholic schools:
Teach French to Polish kids? *'No fools,*
But they've no bent for English'? So?
I'm cool...

I'll say I, too was ESL.
They're all tomorrow's Dux of School:
Lawyers and doctors: I can tell...
They'll hail me on streets: buses full
Who'll swell with pride, to wish me well..

Eid starts today... Let's get beyond
Comment-allez and *Je m'appelle*
Kenzie from Gorgie won't respond.
Won't sit next to *'yon Polish girl'*
(Mum tells her 'Poles are gaun tae Hell')

24 July 2016

Onions

Looking
for my mother
having watched her art-
of cooking things- they mostly must be peeled-
I stole seven onions
from her, seven times
removed rind after rind
skin after skin
till all the skins congealed
and ended in the pedal bin
where nothing was revealed:
an onion with no onion in.
The things I seek remain concealed
within themselves. No grand designs
emerge from matters as they fall apart.
So many skins and casts of mind
later, still no onion heart.
For me, the way's still serpentine,
by stops and starts
on wavy lines;
I know my onions
But my fate's still sealed.
I steer myself
Through roundabouts, round swings
Upsetting onion carts
I see myself
through onion rings
with eyes that smart
looking
for my mother

1994

I'm an Asian Woman but...

I'm an Asian woman but –
Don't patronise me
    categorise me
    finalise me
I'm an Asian woman but
I'm ME

Sorry, I'm not working class
Parents never kept a shop
Didn't leave school at sixteen
Interested, but forced to stop
I'm not what you like to see
I'm ME

Don't have a Midlands accent
Not stamped 'Made in Glasgow'
Bhangra is not my birthright
Hate the Asian talent show
I'm not what you like to hear
I'm ME

Did not apply for Medicine
Or join, ever, Asian Soc
English Lit, yes, not TEFL
Public school, no need to mock
I'm not what you like to promote
I'm ME

Was not forced into marriage
Children? There *are* only two
Dad is not a restaurateur
We manage to make do
I'm not the oppressed wife you think
I'm ME

Caught between two cultures?
No Damn it. That's where *you* are
You've got an ethnic template
I won't get very far.
Because
I'm an Asian woman but –
You can't patronise me
         categorise me
         finalise me
I'm an Asian woman and I'm always
I'm ME

Tariq Latif

Sweet nothings

and when
he learnt of her death
he abandoned the play station
and wandered aimlessly around Priory Woods
and then returned to her gifts,
books by Neruda, Rumi and Tagore.

There was a time
not so long ago
when she had chased him
up the street,
teasing him, kicking him,
laughing as now he stares
down that same echo-less street.

He imagines her funeral pyre
by the Ganges, her lean body
of twenty three
tucked among the hand-picked
branches of mango, cypress
and pomegranate;
her golden hands folded
over his poems
cinnamon sticks
crossed on her breast-bone.

He sets aside the books
and drifts
into wood smoke.

The hollow of her chest
buckles
and the scent of cinnamon
rises
like faint
unfelt kisses ...

The Punjabi Weddings

The cars parked outside the reception hall
range from recent
models of BMW to old Vauxhalls.
Inside, the marriage rites for the decent
groom and bride takes place in separate rooms.
The bride is adorned in a crimson and
gold sari. A dupata hides her face.
Surrounded by women, she thinks the groom's
quarters will be less animated, bland
with dull suits and quieter. The men's pace

is leisurely as they chat and sip Coke
while the molbee
tells the new extended family folk
in both fluent English and Punjabi
that marriage is sacred and not to be
taken lightly. He then utters the vows
in Arabic which the groom repeats word
for musical word. Allah be praised, he
declares and shakes the groom's hand. The groom bows.
The men clap. The groom's dad waits to be heard

and then he invites family and friends
to wish the groom
well and the whole business drags and then ends
with the groom leading the men from the room
to the large dining hall. Basmati rice
from the Punjab is served at weddings in
Glasgow, Manchester, Birmingham, Gravesend
where the adults eat the food rich with spice
as children run round tables in Berlin,
Paris, Rome; speaking Punjabi that sends
hope to the future generations; and

the time has come
for the newly wedded to leave the band
of well-wishers and take the long road home.
The relatives and friends and the in-laws
clear the tables and bin the left-overs;
half-eaten chicken pieces, rice, curry
sauce; a feast for the night creatures with jaws
that will tug at bones. The secret lovers,
fearful of being found, leave in a hurry.

No-one speaks of the indelible stains
of dishonour.
Instead the family goes to great pains
to track them down or pretend the flower
of their lives never existed. The grooms and
brides take off their clothes and work out how to
live their new lives. Their mothers and fathers
sink into chairs and talk of the homeland.
They hope their grand-children arrive on cue.
The girls work the soap that shrinks and lathers.

Walls of Mud

My mouth swallows
the cold-mild air
of in-between seasons.
My fingers glow
like straw in the low light.

I follow my weak,
watery shadow
that falls and floats
over gardens and sea walls.

Some of these holiday homes
are worth over half a million.
How do the owners acquire such wealth?

Someone is cooking porridge.
The warm milky scent
mixes with the smell of damp soil
and my mind is filled
with the mud-made walls
of my grandparents home.
I loved that wholesome living
where everything between life
and death smelt of mud.

I recall the creamy keyre
my grandma used to make,
early winter mornings,
when bars of light
lit the milky steam
from the clay cauldron
(we ate milk-rich rice
with cane sugar

and fine traces of mud;
we worked the land
fed it water
from underground wells
and hand-planted the paddy fields).
I used to imagine
jinns and angels
fighting in the rising steam,
or the beautiful wings
of doves, swans, sea-gulls
sweeping through sunshine,
curlews, sand-pipers and
the two grey herons
wading in the morning tide
next to Bullwood Road.

Shampa Ray

The Man Who Laughs

2 am. He laughs now
to himself, face pink
as he trundles the zimmer.

The parquet living room,
open plan, giggles with him
as never before.

He's on his way
to the downstairs loo again.
Two doors kept open, lights on

for ease of transport.
He laughs all the way there,
this man, my Dad,

and back again to bed,
as though he has saved up
all his joy for the end.

Red Moss

Are you land or water?
You welcome me,
spongy wetland, burnt red
rain-fed mosses stacked
discreetly under heather.
I've gone this way before,

looked out at lochs,
Grand Canyon, a mile deep,
gardens that no longer hang
but are hung into the earth.
I have seen you, cast
my thought-hook elsewhere.

But today it is your
peaty reticence, the silence
of your insects, the lure
of no purchase, that wants me.
Your open-heart surgery landscape
will unravel me enough.

I want your compressed
witness, your tidy files, the human
and inhuman in your dark seams.
What was and is, together,
not reduced like the curlew's cry
but deep as Bible layers.

You do it with such flair,
skip over the ten thousand years.
You are the story I would walk on,
slip through as fish or toad,
come clean to fill your sky
full of bright sentences.

Scent of Memory

I remember the disappointment
of turning a perfect stone to
the side, strewn with moss and dirt.

Dampness lived in the hollow
where stories are told, so
quietly to themselves, we miss them.

A myth by nature is true.
Beetles' trajectory as they scatter
away like the darts of memory.

The pebble is replaced.
Its underside stinks of salt and weed:
print of gathered past.

babs nicgriogair

An Gàidheal
The Pakistani

'underneath the pavement there is the beach' – May 68'

1

anns gach baile brònach
  in every mournful city
fon phavement fhiadhaich
  underneath pavements growing wild
tha tràigh gad ionndrain
  there is a beach that longs for you
bata na do làmh
  a walking stick in your hand
bàta na do sh ilean
  a boat in your eyes

2

neapaicin geal
  a white handkerchief
mar isean air an iteig
  like a bird on the wing
an-dè aig a' phort-adhair
  yesterday at the airport
an-diugh na do phòcaid
  today in your pocket
tha an saoghal a' fàs nas lugha
  the world is growing smaller
's an taigh nas motha
  and the house bigger

tha a' chlann a' fàs mòr
the children are growing up

gad fhàgail le fotos is telebhisean
leaving you with photographs and television

ceann air balla neo air bocsa
a head on a wall or on a box
ann an leabhar neo ann an sgàthan
in a book or in a mirror

cumaidh tu ort, le na soithichean 's le na sgòthan
you will keep on with the dishes and the clouds
an sian nad ch laibh
the rain at your back
seòladair nan speuran
sailor of the skies

3

eadar breith is bàs tha B&B ann an Glaschu
*between the births and deaths there is a B&B in
Glasgow*
eadar prìs chaorach is prìs cruidh tha caitheamh-beatha
*between the price of sheep and that of cattle there is a
livelihood*
eadar clach is cladh tha cuimhne
between a stone and a grave there is a memory

4

tha goirt san tìr
famine is in the land
is pian nad amhaich

   and a pain in your throat
tha blas cànain
   the taste of a language
fhathast air do theanga
   lingers on the tongue
's an t-acras ort
   and you are hungry

5

le leac-aughach an àite cluasaig
   with a tombstone for a pillow
chan fhaigh thu mòran cadail
   you won't get much sleep

6

air do ghlùinean ann an cidsin
   on your knees in a kitchen
neo ann an achadh
   or in a field
ach seasaidh do chreideamh
   with your faith still standing.

Nalini Paul

Deluge

Rain sprattles the slate rooftops
  slides along drainpipes
  sheeting the streets like a mirror.

A charcoal evening in Stromness
the brightest shade repeated on flagstones
echoed at pierheads
and wave-quenched houses.

The sea hides in a blur of clouds
a pale blue promise unfolding to calm.

Seals periscope the surface
as the sky pours out its tears.

'Cat, yaar'

It was nothing then
to let go of the cat
onto carpet or concrete
from windows or beds.

Sink your hands deep
   into black fur
and grasp the velvet-purr warmth...

My palette was cleansed of chicken curry
with a mouthful of frozen blueberries.
No scent of cumin or cardamom came
like Burramummy's breath after dinner

or fish and dhal rolled into rice balls
kofta parcelled in soft chapattis
as my mother's fingers popping them in.

Beef pillao with basmati rice
green chillies cooled with raitha.

Chicken bones chewed
the marrow sucked out
tandoori-bright red
like make-believe blood.

Now the lustre slips with the years
and it is harder to drop
that living creature
licking its chops
or shielding eyes from the sun
with its paws.

Companion with a secret language
the one that has my tongue.

yaar (Hindi) – friend, my friend.
Burramummy (Hindi) – grandmother

Eight miles of weather

Horizontal snow –
stag apparitions
walk to Torridon.

Fungi, Dawyck Botanical Gardens

Hairy curtain crust
Turkey tail
Sulphur tuft

Arisaig

Green eyes
wink
in cardigan sea.

Surge

The tide yawns in and out
of the sea loch
yearns and moves
to wider expanses.

Language drowns.

Then sound emerges
    a waterlogged bell
    washed with the cathedral.

Our differences settle into stained glass
fragments form an image

voices sing.

We write each line of a sonnet
in water
shaping a welcome out of clarity
    light
    chatter
    trout
    heather

Black-and-white
    passes us
  slips and fades

That monochrome way
    of seeing is gone

The husk of our remembering
    raises the sun
and colours are born.

Shadows in Colour

The house lights go down
and mobiles switch off.
Are we in this together?

In that lilac dream
where we never meet,
lovers or enemies make chance encounters.
But the same window frames our desire:
shadows, colour and light
play tricks with the eye.
As you watch all the destinies you may never visit
make the journey, starry eyed
every frame a memory of some other place
myths are created with every foreign face...
We copy, they mimic
from Arabia to India.
Echo wears their jewels in her crown.
And up and down the country

we watch blackened faces
speak in accents that trip off the tongue.
The aisles burst with laughter
but some can't even fathom the distance.
So questions form like little flames:
why does my heart dance
at the apparition,
shapes that will never know me by name?
Sitting here in the dark
where no colours exist
boundaries shouldn't cross us.
Yet even in this gazing
what do you see?

The camera lies.
Then something stirs in the pool of thought
some swell of mystery catches each sigh.

Arré yaar, look at me
and don't turn away:
I'm only your reflection.

Note:
Arré (Hindi) – 'hey' or 'come on, now'
Yaar (Hindi) – friend, my friend

Lay Down Your Head

Velvet forest bed
scatters shadows of branches:
dream its ghostly breeze.

Sunset Over Gairloch

The orange light melted
rich like toffee,
sad like time's stuck surface.

Dream-like

Floating haystacks
drop dream shapes
into the mind's cubbyholes.

Twitching

A crow like a falling blow-tie flies,
guilty party with cheese in beak:
a seagull dive-bombs pursuit.
Coal-black creature does a shoulder check,
a flapping panic of soot.

A moorhen cranks a cry at a squirrel
insulting anything grey
that threatens its pond-walk swim.

A swan stands ankle-deep
in the dying low-lying river,
beaking its plumes in search of words
when a robin ripens on a branch of hazel.

Its partner approaches,
a counterpoint of

red
    and
            brown
    brown
and
red
    and
red
   and
brown.

Hamid Shami

Lost

To quote my distant friend Imran MacLeod,
'A man with no culture has no identity.'

The last I heard from him was, he was off
To the Himalayas.

He had a very confused childhood.

Father was Scottish,
Mother Pakistani.

They'd always be arguing over many things
Concerning him.

One was religion.

Father wanted him brought up
A Catholic; mother wanted a Muslim.

Was the only boy on our street who went
To mosque on Fridays and chapel on Sundays.

But in the mountains

God's sure to find him.

Just Schools

Good to know
That all our great teachers
Are
White lower middle class
Loving

Christians.

Animal Impersonations

Dog –
woof woof

Cow –
moo

Skinhead
fuckin' – black – bastard.

Mother Tongue

Yes,
I speak
Fluent
Urdu
But
In my dreams
I bawl,
Curse
And swear
In the
Queen's
English.

For Starters

Love
Indian, Chinese
And Italian too.

Race is
Not an issue
With me

So long as
The service
And food

Are good.

Raman Mundair

Sheep Hill, Fair Isle

I begin sheepishly,
   feel with fingers
attempt to roo

your softness taut
in struggle. I soothe
         with lullaby

you settle. In no time
at all the shear's song
reveals your baby skin

   you free yourself
of me. Hoof it away. My fingers
lanolin soft with your memory.

Irfan Merchant

National Colours

I

The teams picked and lined-up in rank,
we jogged onto the school football pitch
like iambs on a sonnet's green rectangle,
limbering-up for the big metre.
There we were, high with the fresh
juice of adolescence in our shorts –
the keen ones, jittering like wound-up
clockwork toys, in Scotland strips;
my kit was from *What Every Woman Wants*.

The rhythm of the game settled itself
as the ball was passed along the wing
in an *a-b-a-b* rhyming scheme.
Then: '*Up the Pairk!*' bellows Mr Phillips
the PE teacher, and so a boy belters the ball,
soaring, opening up the field: *On Yersel
Big Man!*' But it's intercepted by the defence,
as the sestet turns the game around,
finishing with a nifty headered couplet.

Always the odd one out, I was busy
watching the steam spout from my lips
as I walked slowly between the goals,
a caesura through the classical mould. Then:
'*Eerie-Fanny Get Yer Arse In Gear!*'
(Or it was *Earwig, Irvine, Fanny-Face*; or
Paki-Bastard, Shoe-Shine Boy, Get Back Home:
the mysterious dervish name from Persia

whirled on the thick-set tongue of Ayrshire).
Minded of Ghandi's epic salt march
I kept on my measured pace
quietly disrupting the maths of the game;
and by the final whistle,
my boots were as muddy as the rest.

II

At home, football was just not cricket;
my dad wanted me to bat for India
or England, depending who was beating Pakistan.
'When in Rome, do as the Romans do'
was his mantra, and as the history master
at St Peter's European Boys School,
Panchgani, taught him by rote
the Kings and Queens of England
and the civil order of innings and over,

we were the Romans in a Pictish town.
So at Cambusdoon Cricket Club
I polished spin bowling weekly,
mastering the wily Oriental 'googly'.
And my dad has a photo of me framed
in a V-neck pullover and long white trousers
with green and orange stains;
feet clasped, knees just bent
and a bat posed forever at my toes:
I peer out from a pudding-bowl fringe
as if still batting at the crease;
waiting for the next bowl
like an Indian boy
who knows his place.

I'm a Racist

'If this is a paki, a darkie and a chinky, you're a racist.'
– *slogan on a poster produced by the City of Edinburgh
Council, with three appropriate head-and-shoulder photos.*

I saw a paki
on the side of a bus.

I'm a paki.

I thought to myself:

How nice. A paki
on the side of a bus.

Address Tae Chicken Tikka Masala

Fair fa' the nation's favourite dish
fulfilling everybody's wish,
great chieftain, O so very Scottish,
          the spice o life;
ye came, and conquered the English,
          tae cure the strife.

Born in Glasgow's Shish Mahal
during Thatcher's iron rule,
your origins stretch to the Mughals
          but when they tried
the chicken tikka, the locals
          found it too dry.

The chef wad think tae open up
a can o' Campbell's tomato soup,
add chilli, colouring with pap-
          -rika for zest;
and then, O what a glorious sup,
          simply the best.

As Scots we want the hottest thing
on the menu, a dish with zing:
haggis disnae mak us sing –
          we're globalised;
it's the mince an tatties o Tony Singh
          brings tears tae eyes.

Noo we export tae India
oor national dish, making it clear
that Scotland is a warld leader
                    in aa the airts;
fir chicken tikka masala
                      ye've won oor hairts.

Lord Ganesh, tae please the Scots
remember whit they want is lots
o sauce and spices, very hot,
                    but dinnae worry;
Ah've got the answer in ma pot –
                  gie them a curry.

The Other Arthur's Seat

...till they came under the English Government
they have not been accustomed to assert the nose upon
their face their own... This temper prevails,
more or less, in the converted.—Rev. Mr Corrie

Le nez de Cleopatre: s'il eut ete plus court,
toute la face de la terre aurait change.—Blaise Pascal

I have it in mind: the vertiginous drop,
the green Konkan plain below; between me
and thin air, a thin wooden platform, creaking
on the edge of a cliff. Somehow it would last
all those years that we made our exile's return,
pilgrims of beauty spots, cousins, and aunts,
our family more peopled than even a peepul tree
whose dreadlocked long branches grow back to the earth
becoming the roots of a younger tree...
And no less of a puzzle to me, even though
we all share in common a nose, our birthright
passed down through the ages; the Rajabali Nose,
a landmark that's travelled the world and back.

Now it's back we will travel, a voyage to that ledge
up in the ghats, off the end of the line;
the breathtaking fall and the quivering boards,
a typically Hindu construction, you might say;
to my eyes precarious, but somehow balanced
as is a jug on a young woman's head
as she walks down the road, poised and radiant...

*

Half-on and half-off the tourist circuit,
around the same route every three or four years
like circling the Ka'ba, or beads of a mala:
the flight into Santa Cruz (Bombay) airport,
the heat and the dust of the road through the slums
to Uncle Shums' flat for sweet lime, or sweetened sour lime;
a whistle-stop tour, buzzing in rickshaws –
Juhu, Marine Drive, the Gateway, the Taj
InterContinental Hotel; then the train up to Poona
which halts at each station for cashew-nut brittle
and bottles of cold drinks – Gold Spot and Thums-Up
and Limca – while chai-wallahs walk through the carriages
chanting *chai-chai, chai-chai, chai-chai;*
then on in a taxi which, by some miracle,
climbs the steep hairpin loops into Panchgani
to Chishtia Manzil, our home in the hills...
And maybe I don't understand or know why
we'll shudder, one day, in an old station wagon,
a yellow and black boneshaker, to stop dead
at a lake for tiffin, as the British would say –
stainless steel canisters packed with pakora,
green coconut chutni sandwiched in chapati;
after, at Hotel Happy Home, masala chai
so sweet, your nose will wrinkle
as you pour it discreetly into a pot plant.

The day-trip will take us next to Mahabaleshwar
where Shivaji tore apart Afzar Khan
with his tiger claws. Where, in a dark, damp temple
the source of the Krishna flows from a stone cow.
The British came here, for summers of governance;
the cool of the hills they'd tour and discover
and rename each place for its view, shape or finder:
Kate's Point, Babington Point, Chinaman's Falls –
replacing each myth with history.
Soon, our excursion must end with the jaunt

to Arthur's Seat: on the narrow cliff-path
past Tiger Spring, to the rickety shelf
on the brink, as I said, just thin air and planks
with gaps the wind whistles through; a sheer drop
in the sky, hundreds, thousands of feet.

Crowding on, seemingly careless of heights,
the locals lean on the wobbly handrail
for the view to the west coastal flats.

*

I thought this would go on forever, a lifetime;
the same wagon, same photos, the family line-up
in front of my ancient grandparents, timeless
as India Herself...
                              But now
that I've reached this shaky cliff-hanger
there's only one way to go, which is forwards
off the precipice, tumbling
                                        into the void
                     mid-air
                                   the mind's magic carpet
appears out of nothing and slips through a flaw
in the fabric of time – as a hand-woven rug
with one man-made loop-hole – which seems to have
brought us
to where this began: this room with a view
of the *other* Arthur's Seat,
in Edinburgh.
                     Asleep in the grass,
the extinct volcano, viewed eastwards
a crouching lion.

*

Somewhere, in the distance, I hear her, the Deccan Queen
gathering speed for her royal descent
from the heavenly heights to Victoria Terminus:
O Romance Of Steam! O Engine Of History!
Come chattering out the black mouth of a tunnel
then gallop away through the ghats like a dream,
Victorian Triumph Of Rail Engineering
trailing steam back, an unravelling shroud
releasing its ghosts to the sky...
                                        Or is that
just a trick of memory, that steam? So much
might be footage from *Jewel In The Crown*
or *Passage To India* . . . the tiffin,
the 'Hindu construction'...
The scene fades away, though the soundtrack repeats
as her wheels, like a loop-tape, thump over the points;
hammering on through the stations and cuttings
their steel incantation, the Deccan Queen's English
echoing down through the years to me now:

*...Parsee Point – Bombay Point – Sidney Point – Wilson
Point –
Tiger Spring – Tableland – Arthur's Seat – Duke's Nose...*

The Director's Cut

The camera pans along Edinburgh's skyline,
the Castle, the Mile, Calton Hill, the Crags,
reveals Arthur's Seat as a slumbering lion
who suddenly wakens, a long-buried roar
quaking the crust along its fault lines;
the lion is rising and turning towards us
his gorse-yellow mane, his opening jaw
the yawn of a mouth approaching: at the point
where this track will vanish in darkness,
the hole in the hill swallowing us whole
into the belly of magma and lava
the scene will distort, involute, to emerge
inside out, downside up, as the great Deccan Queen
comes rumbling out an intestinal tunnel
then gallops away, a wild mare, through the ghats,
her white tail an unravelling spool . . .
O Steam Allegory! O Engine Necessity!
O Wheel's Inexorable Shunt!

The sleepers lie still in the weight of the ballast
and history runs on those same iron rails,
the parallel balance of fate and desire
which seems to resolve in a bright speck of nothing
upon the horizon we cannot attain
as the tall shadow working the dark signal-box
on the late shift, swilling tea, still on track,
is crossing the points and shifting the levers,
 resetting the signals, her wide amber eyes
in which we are trapped now like dust, like flies.

Masala Child

Not just any mixture
but the right combination,
though if you want the recipe

you'll hear the usual thing –
a bit of this, a bit of that;
you're meant to understand.

Not blended, but unified
as yoga, each element
distinct, yet integrated.

Chai-coloured child,
his heart infused with India,
her sweetness, her secret ingredients.

Tryst

Beyond ideas of yes and no
there is a field where wildflowers grow –

a wish-fulfilling cow lives there
grazing on a silent prayer;

her form is full of every bliss,
her beauty is the truth we miss;

her radiance shines as our sun,
the source of life for everyone;

our moon, our cycle of rebirth,
her face turning towards our earth

blessing all lovers in their tryst
with destiny in every kiss;

she saunters on her milky way
as starchildren come out to play

upon that field where wildflowers grow
beyond ideas of yes and no.

Sarbojit Biswas

One Step and Another

Again and again up a flight
I rise
In darkness
For the next landing, the next light.
I hear voices
Faint
Fellow climbers
But I rise, alone
Towards light.
I am there, here
In a flush of midday sun
A tongue of cold breeze
Floating over a city.
Days back I had risen
Crossed the skies
On a bird
To your land
From where you came to mine.
You came to me in pages
I read you
With childish wonder
Your lines daunted
But I rose
I climbed as I am climbing now.
Saw light
Understood you –
Did I?
For darkness envelopes
Another flight
Another trudge
Laborious and silent.

The wait to know
The wait to climb
The wait to achieve
Started in my land
Ends in yours.
For you I aspired
For you I climb
Of you I read
On your memorial I climb.
I perspired in darkness
Into cool light I enter again
The second level? (As in a video game?)
This is not a game
Another level onward
Another flight
Game on
Last light.
Bright light
Your city again
I see your station
Your highlands
Your hero
Revolution
My pent up desires.
I traversed the sky on a bird
Climbed to touch your sky
Your sky loves me now
Your pages beckon still
I remember my heroes
You have your own
I still remain small
On top
On the Scott memorial
In Edinburgh.

Subhadeep Paul

Scotbuds

You knew beforehand that I would like Aberdeen Angus,
Langoustines, Atlantic Salmon, the spoils of creameries
And the Scottish cheddar of Campbeltown.
You had stockpiles shelved for me
By Bute, Arran, Mull and Orkney.

You transported me to a timeless realm
Where Scottish soldiers fed visitors from their sacks of oatmeal.
You know I'm eyes wide open
For a Burns Supper, which is what you promised me.

Overtime, I took a fancy for haggis, neeps and tatties
You know, my friend, you won my heart
With Scotch and Orkney cheddar
Which made even cognac take the backseat!
Let's toast to the 'water of life' today!
* * *

Ten years later in a Michelin-starred Tokyo restaurant
Your Scotbuds were missing me.

Notes on the Authors

Frances Ainslie (b.1958) Born in Govan, Frances Ainslie is a short story writer and poet and is currently writing her first novel. Her short stories have won a number of prizes and in 2017 she won the Dunedin (New Zealand) Burns Prize (unpublished poet). She graduated from the University of Stirling in 2015 with an MLitt in Creative Writing and is now studying towards a Masters in Scottish Literature. Frances worked in Global IT for 30 years and frequently travelled to India. The country and its people captured her heart and continue to inspire her writing.

Deb Narayan Bandyopadhyay (b.1954) is Vice Chancellor, Bankura University, West Bengal, India, the Secretary of the Indian Association of Scottish Studies, and formerly Professor in the Department of English, Burdwan University, India. He visited the University of Edinburgh and lectured at a seminar organised at Mansfield College, Oxford in 2002, with assistance from the British Council. He has occupied many prestigious scholarly positions internationally and is the author of numerous scholarly books and articles. His poems have been published in various journals in India.

Jane Bhandari (b.1944) Born in Edinburgh, educated in England, Bhandari has lived in India for over 40 years, mainly in Mumbai, formerly Bombay. A poet and painter, her poems are published in *Single Bed* and *Aquarius*. She has written stories for children and has been active in a poetry reading group in Mumbai, 'Loquations'. The painterly detail in her poems, with which she evokes visual textures and especially the subtle relations of colours, belies any simple sense of national identity, Scottish, British or Indian. Rather, her poems enact both sensual precision and personal engagement with the material and immaterial world.

Sheena Blackhall (b.1947). Born in Aberdeen, Blackhall is a poet, novelist, short story writer, artist, children's author and traditional story teller and singer. Honorary Research Associate of the Elphinstone Institute at Aberdeen University and appointed Makar for the city of Aberdeen in 2009, Blackhall keenly promotes Scots culture and language in the North East of Scotland.

Sarbojit Biswas (b.1976) Born in Durgapur, the Ruhr of India, Sarbojit Biswas grew up among towering factory chimneys and tall trees, planned urbanity and resplendent nature. Today, he teaches English and Scottish literature at Bankura University in India and writes poetry on growing up, celebrating his experiences roaming the world and knowing himself as he ages.

Ian Brown (b.1945) is a Scottish poet, playwright and scholar. He has been, *inter alia*, Scottish Society of Playwrights Chair, Arts Council of Great Britain Drama Director, Queen Margaret University Dean of Arts, Association for Scottish Literary Studies President and Saltire Society Convener. He was the general editor of the three-volume *Edinburgh History of Scottish Literature* (Edinburgh University Press, 2006) and his poems are collected in *Collyshangles in the Canopy* (Kilkerran: Kennedy & Boyd, 2015).

Bashabi Fraser (b.1954 in India). Professor of English and Creative Writing and co-founder and Director of the Scottish Centre of Tagore Studies (ScoTs) at Edinburgh Napier University. Her recent publications include *The Homing Bird* (2017), *Ragas & Reels* (2012), *Scots Beneath the Banyan Tree: Stories from Bengal* (2012); *From the Ganga to the Tay* (2009); *Bengal Partition Stories: An Unclosed Chapter* (2006; 2008), *A Meeting of Two Minds: the Geddes Tagore Letters* (2005) and *Tartan & Turban* (2004). Her awards include Outstanding Woman of Scotland, Saltire Society; Rabindra Bharati Society Honour for promoting Tagore Studies in Europe, 2014; Women Empowered: Arts and Culture Award, 2010.

Valerie Gillies (b.1948) is the author of eight books of poetry. Commonwealth Scholar at the University of Mysore 1970–1971; Creative Scotland Award 2005; Edinburgh Makar 2005–2008; Associate of Harvard University, 2009–2015. Valerie facilitates the Creative Writing groups at Maggie's Cancer Centre, Edinburgh. Her most recent book is *The Cream of the Well: New and Selected Poems* (Edinburgh: Luath, 2015).

James Ross Hutchinson (1796–1870) served for 20 years as a surgeon on the Bengal Establishment, secretary to the Medical Board of the Calcutta Presidency, and private secretary to the president of the Council of India, then retired to South Africa. He had collected his poems there in 1837. He was a champion of medical reform, especially regarding hygiene in hospitals and prisons. In his poem, 'The Sunyassee or Pilgrim of India' the hero compares rising English power to a 'vast Upas tree' spreading poison everywhere.

Violet Jacob (1863–1946) Born into the landed family of Kennedy-Erskine, Violet married a soldier, travelling with him to India, South Africa and Egypt, returning in 1904. After their one son was killed in the First World War, she lived on as a lady in the House of Dun, near Montrose, an aristocrat, to that extent, but far closer to less well-off people than most of today's richest. As well as her poems, her novels *Flemington* and *The Interlopers* are well worth reading. See also *Diaries and Letters from India 1895–1900*, edited by Carol Anderson (Edinburgh: Canongate, 1990) and *Voices From Their Ain Countrie: The Poems of Marion Angus and Violet Jacob*, edited by Katherine Gordon (Glasgow: Association for Scottish Literary Studies, 2006).

Rudyard Kipling (1865–1936) Kipling's father, John Lockwood Kipling, was a sculptor and Principal and Professor of Architecture at the newly founded Sir Jamsetjee Jeejebhoy School of Art in

Bombay, and his mother, Alice, was born a MacDonald, one of four equally remarkable sisters, a vivacious woman of whom it was said that dullness could not exist with her in the same room. His parents referred to themselves as Anglo-Indians though Anglo-Indian-Scots might be more accurate for Kipling's mother and himself. Born in Bombay, Kipling was educated in England, returning to India as a newspaperman and writer. Despite the notoriety he has in some quarters as a child of Empire and carrier of its prejudices and disposition, he remains stylistically brilliant, not least in *The Jungle Books*, the *Just So Stories* and such short fiction as 'The Man Who Would Be King'.

Tariq Latif (b.1962) Born and grew up in a small farming village outside Lahore, Pakistan, his family moved to Manchester in 1970 when he was eight years old. He graduated from Sheffield University with a degree in Physics and was involved in the family printing business for 15 years before moving to Argyll. He has had a passion for poetry for over 30 years and enjoys rambling, writing, reading and cooking, and works in a call centre to keep the wolf at bay.

John Leyden (1775–1811) Born in the Scottish Borders, Leyden studied divinity in Edinburgh. When becoming a Church of Scotland minister proved impossible, the Church supported him to cram a course in medical science and go to India as an assistant surgeon to the East India Company in Madras. His knowledge of at least six, possibly nine, languages was extraordinary and informed his intellectual enquiries on his travels through South India, Malaysia and Java. He became a judge in rural Bengal and an assay master of the Calcutta mint. His first published book was a long poem, *Scenes of Infancy, Descriptive of Teviotdale* (1803). By character a Scots divine, he was appalled by both 'pagan' religions and rabid commercialism.

Liz Lochhead (b.1947) Born in Craigneuk, a wee village near Motherwell in Lanarkshire, Lochhead went to the Glasgow School of Art, 1965–70 and became a schoolteacher before her first book

Memo for Spring was published in 1972, and a new voice was heard loud and clear in the Scottish literary arena. She has lived in Glasgow for many years, happily married to the architect Tom Logan until his untimely death in 2010. In 2005 she was appointed as the Glasgow Poet Laureate and from 2011–16 she was the Scots Makar, in both cases immediately following Edwin Morgan. Her many books of poems have appeared alongside her plays, seminal work such as *Mary Queen of Scots Got Her Head Chopped Off* (2001) and her translation of Euripides's *Medea* (2000). The poem published here is from her first book, where it appeared under a different title. It is characteristic of two major themes that run through all her work: neighbourliness, and different voices.

Christine De Luca (b. 1947) Born in Shetland, De Luca moved to Edinburgh to study, works there as an educationalist and has been the Edinburgh Makar or poet laureate. She writes in both English and Shetlandic. Her collection *Wast wi da Valkyries* was published by The Shetland Library in 1997, and was awarded the Shetland Literary Prize.

Peter McCarey (b.1956) Born in Paisley and brought up in Glasgow, he retired from his post as Chief Translator for the World Health Organization in Geneva, where he has lived for many years. His poems are published in *Collected Contraptions* (Manchester: Carcanet, 2011) and his online epic *The Syllabary* can be found at: http://www.thesyllabary.com / http://www.cleikit. com. His critical work is published in *Hugh MacDiarmid and the Russians* (Edinburgh: Scottish Academic Press, 1988) and *Find and Angel and Pick a Fight* (Geneva: Molecular Press, 2013).

Hugh MacDiarmid (C.M. Grieve) (1892–1978) Major 20th-century poet. That Rudyard Kipling became Lord Rector of St Andrews University in the same year the name Hugh MacDiarmid was first seen in print, the same year as the publication of *Ulysses* and *The Waste Land*, the same year that a British colonial court sentenced Gandhi to six years' imprisonment for sedition after a protest march led to violence in Bombay, overlaps modernism with the legacy of the British Empire and India's struggle for independence in a chronology that dissolves the security of firm divisions. Born in Langholm, a small town twelve miles from the border with England, MacDiarmid, or Christopher Murray Grieve, lived in most parts of Scotland, from the major cities to the northernmost archipelago of Shetland. He travelled to America, Canada, the Eastern Bloc countries and China, but he never visited India. However, his writings on India are far more extensive than one might suspect. See the indispensable critical essay 'India in Hugh MacDiarmid's Poetry' by Ramkrishna Bhattacharya, available online.

Irfan Merchant was born in Liverpool in 1973 of Indian descent. From the age of three months he was brought up in Ayr and lives there. His poems have appeared in various magazines and in *The Redbeck Anthology of British South Asian Poetry* (Redbeck, 2000).

Aonghas Moireasdan / Angus Morrison (1865–1942) Born in Ullapool, son of a shoemaker, Morrison became a tea and coffee merchant, moved to Inverness and was secretary and treasurer of the Gaelic Society there, c.1904–07. He seems to have travelled throughout Scotland collecting songs and pipe tunes. When he died in Edinburgh, he was vice-president of the Highland Pipers' Society. There is no evidence that he ever visited India but his poem, 'Thoughts on the Greatness of the British Empire' is pertinent to the central themes of the political history from which the present anthology arises.

Edwin Morgan (1920–2010) Major 20th-century poet. Like MacDiarmid, Morgan was far-travelled but never to India. His Indian poems, like much of his best work, arise from his research and imagination. Morgan was a Professor of English at Glasgow University, the first Glasgow poet laurate and the first Scots Makar, or national bard. His breakthrough volume was *The Second Life* (1968) and as well as numerous books of poems, including the seminal *Sonnets from Scotland* (1984) and *Cathures* (2002), he wrote plays, including *A.D.: A Trilogy on the Life of Jesus Christ* (2000) and *Gilgamesh* (2005), song lyrics, critical essays, literary reviews and maintained an international correspondence, all before emails and online technology were available.

Raman Mundair Born in Ludhiana, India, Mundair came to Britain in the 1970s at the age of five. Her poems are collected in *A Choreographer's Cartography* and *Lovers, Liars, Conjurers and Thieves*. She is also a playwrite with *The Algebra of Freedom* (produced by 7:84 Theatre Company) and *Side Effects*, a one-act play (produced in collaboration with the National Theatre Scotland Young Company and Òran Mòr in their 'A Play, A Pie, and A Pint' series). She is also an author of short stories with *In the Light of Other* and in 2006 and as an artist she blends texts and narratives in visual forms. Her work has been exhibited at the Gallery of Modern Art, Glasgow, City Art Gallery, Leicester and Kevin Kavanagh Gallery, Dublin.

Jameela Muneer (b.1961) Born in Hyderabad, moved to the UK when she was five. She grew up in Wales, studied at the Universities of London (Royal Holloway College), Strathclyde, and Edinburgh. She has been a broadcaster, teacher and lawyer. She has taught Creative Writing and collaborates with Scottish musicians in setting her poems to music and performing at literary events. She lives in Edinburgh.

babs nicgriogair (b.1967) Born on the Isle of Lewis in the summer of love, babs nicgrigair is a native Gaelic speaker. She describes herself as a peace activist and 'landscape artist', and has in the past 'waited on tables, turned tables, pulled pints and pushed Penguins'. She works with writing, visual arts and theatre.

Nalini Paul (b.1968) Nalini Paul is a widely published poet whose work explores her mixed heritage: born in India, she grew up in Canada and has been living in Scotland for most of her adult life. Her collaborations with visual artists, dancers, musicians and actors have been staged in Orkney, Glasgow and Edinburgh. She is currently working on her first full collection. www.nalinipaul.com

Subhadeep Paul (b.1980) Born in Kolkata, Paul received part of his early schooling in Dr. Graham's Homes, a boarding school founded by the revered Scottish Missionary John Anderson Graham in Kalimpong, North Bengal. At Bankura University where he currently teaches as an Assistant Professor in the Department of English, he conducts a Special Optional Paper on Scottish Literature. His poetry, short stories and non-fictional works have appeared in numerous forums such as *8th Day (The Sunday Statesman)*, *The Telegraph*, *Earthen Lamp Journal*, *The Four Quarters Magazine*, *Blue Minaret*, *North East Review*, *Edi-Blossom* (from Edinburgh). His selected poems are in *Finite Sketches, Infinite Reaches* (Kolkata: Writers' Workshop, 2007). He is currently working on a novel he describes as a 'three-generation family quest saga'.

John Purser (b.1947) is a Scottish composer, musicologist, music historian, playwright and poet. His book *Scotland's Music* (Edinburgh: Mainstream, 1992; new edition October 2007) is a major reference work on Scotland's musical history from the Bronze Age to the present. It was based on his 30 50–minute–programme radio series of the same title, broadcast on BBC Radio Scotland. His radio plays include the Giles Cooper Award-winning *Carver*, about Robert Carver, the brilliant 16th-century Scottish composer of choral church music. His poems are published in *There Is No Night: New and Selected Poems* (Kilkerran: Kennedy & Boyd, 2014). http://www.johnpurser.net/

Tessa Ransford (1938–2015) Born in India, educated in Scotland, Tessa Ransford spent eight years in Pakistan as the wife of a Church of Scotland missionary and returned then to Scotland to become the founding Director of the Scottish Poetry Library in Edinburgh, which opened in 1984, and the editor of the poetry magazine *Lines Review* from 1988–98. Ali Smith has written that in her poems one finds 'the enlightened mind at work, at both art and the problems of the world, rich with native wit, keen to connect and transform.'

Ransford herself has written: 'India and Scotland are entwined like a Kashmir shawl round my life. The knot cannot be unravelled but can uncoil like a snake, start up the brain-fever-bird that disturbs any chance of rest.' See *Indian selection: poems* (Kirkcaldy: Akros Publications, 2000) and *Not Just Moonshine: new and selected poems* (Edinburgh: Luath Press, 2008).

Shampa Ray (b.1967) Born in New Delhi, Shampa Ray grew up in a village in Renfrewshire, Scotland. She also spent a brief part of her childhood living in Baghdad, Iraq. She is a visual artist working in Edinburgh. Her poetry has been published widely in anthologies including: *Wish I Was Here* (Pocketbooks); *Making Waves* (Federation of Writers Scotland); *Out of Bounds* (Bloodaxe) and exhibited in 'Mists and Monsoons' at the Writers' Museum, Edinburgh. She speaks Bengali and English. She has published in *Fox, Wellspring, Spectrum* and ALP publications. Shampa currently lives in Kirkcudbrightshire.

Alan Riach (b.1957) is the Professor of Scottish Literature at Glasgow University. Born in Airdrie, Lanarkshire, after taking his first degree from Cambridge in 1979, completed a PhD in Scottish Literature at the University of Glasgow in 1986 and worked in New Zealand at the University of Waikato, 1986–2000. He is the author of numerous books and articles, including *Hugh MacDiarmid's Epic Poetry* (1991), *Representing Scotland in Literature, Popular Culture and Iconography* (2005) and the co-author with Alexander Moffat of *Arts of Resistance: Poets, Portraits and Landscapes of Modern Scotland* (2009), described by the *Times Literary Supplement* as 'a landmark book' and *Arts of Independence: The Cultural Argument and Why It Matters Most* (2014). His sixth book of poems, *The Winter Book* (2017), follows *Homecoming* (2009), *Clearances* (2001), *First & Last Songs* (1995), *An Open Return* (1991) and *This Folding Map* (1990).

David Lester Richardson (1801–65) has been described by the scholar Mary Ellis Gibson as 'the single most influential teacher of British literature in 19th-century India' who was 'among the first to publish Indian poets writing in English' and who 'did much to encourage literary English in Bengal' where he was in military service until invalided out. He then became a professor of English and principal of Hindu College, then of Krishnanagar College and Hugli College near Calcutta. As an editor, publisher, anthologist as well as poet and teacher, his influence was extensive. Born in London, his wife and family remained there and he returned frequently, so the divided loyalties of an enthusiasm for and commitment to India and his vocation, and his pleasure in and loyalty to the priorities of domesticity characterise his work. As an English poet, he is included here on the grounds that his poems have clear affinities with those of other British expatriates and a direct connection to the Burns tradition, as much as that of Wordsworth and Milton. Their themes are central and help reconfigure any simple or singular ideas of national identity.

Coinneach Ros / Rev. Kenneth Ross (1914–90) Born in Glendale, Skye, eldest of eleven children from a crofting family, from 1935–45 he served as a Warrant Officer with the Royal Air Force in India, Burma and other places. After the Second World War, he became the minister of the islands of Gigha and Cara, and later Lismore and Northmavine in Shetland. He married the Northumbrian artist Mary Parker and when he retired in 1980, they moved there.

Suhayl Saadi (b.1961) Born in Yorkshire in, six years after his parents arrived from Pakistan, Suhayl was brought up in Glasgow where he now lives and works as a doctor. His books include *The Snake* (1997), *The Burning Mirror* (2001), *Psychoraag* (2004), *The White Cliffs* (2005) and *Joseph's Box* (2009) and he has worked with radio and stage and on various poetry commissions. He was British Council writer-in-residence at George Washington University. His poems and short stories have appeared in various magazines as well as *Macallan Shorts 1999* published by Polygon. His novel *Psychoraag* (2004) won a PEN Oakland/Josephine Miles Literary Award and the National Literary Award in Pakistan, and was one of the Scottish Book Trust's '100 Best Scottish Books of All Time'. It was described by Angus Calder as *'Midnight's Children* meets *Trainspotting.'*

Chrys Salt (b.1944) is a trained performer and broadcaster as well as a widely published and anthologized poet. She has read her work across the UK in Europe, The USA, Canada, Finland and India and has won numerous awards. In 2014 she was awarded an MBE in the Queen's Birthday Honours List for Services to The Arts and is listed in *Who's Who*. www.chryssalt.com

Walter Scott (1771–1832) Novelist, poet, playwright, editor, anthologist, advocate, judge, legal administrator, Scott was friendly or acquainted with almost all the literary and cultural figures of his era in Britain and internationally, and was read by an unquantifiable number of people worldwide. An advocate of the work and career of John Leyden (see above), Leyden helped collect work for Scott when he was editing the *Minstrelsy of the Scottish Border* (1802–03). Scott went on to write historical novels from *Waverley* (1814) to *Castle Dangerous* (1832) that revolutionised literature internationally. He wrote best about the country he knew, but his novels set in places he never visited are of considerable interest, as he explains in the 'Prefatory' to *The Surgeon's Daughter* (1827). Prose fiction as it is, it defines an ambiguity essential to poetry: we sometimes reach truths through writing from experience, but in literature, truths are also the children of the imagination. If this opening extract from *The Surgeon's Daughter* might be read as an exposé of exploitation and charlatanism, it also might suggest that we don't always know where what we do will take us, for better or worse. That's surely true of so many people involved in Scottish / British / Indian / South Asian relations, literary, cultural, commercial and political, since at least the early 19th century.

Vikram Seth (b.1952) Born in Kolkata, Seth went to school first in India, then in England, and studied philosophy, politics and economics in London, completing a PhD in economics at Stanford, USA. He led the campaign against the law against homosexuality in India in 2006. At 1,349 pages, his novel *A Suitable Boy* (1993) was a major literary event, as was the following novel, *An Equal Music* (1999). Seth's published poetry includes *Mappings* (1980), *At Evening* (1993) and *Summer Requiem* (2012).

Hamid Shami (b.1969) Born in Pakistan, brought up in Glasgow, Shami is a frequent contributor to *Scotland's Oracle*, an independent multicultural newspaper.

Gerry Singh (b. 1957) Born in Glasgow, Gerry Singh describes his family background as unknown, his Scottish identity as 'deeply hidden within', and his Indian roots as 'painted on my face'. The poems included in this collection reflect a period of work directly concerned with these issues of identity and dislocation, while more recent work shows a growing interest in landscape. He is now a teacher in Perthshire. His poetry is featured in *The Redbeck Anthology of British South Asian Poetry.*

Alan Spence (b.1947) is an award-winning Scottish poet and playwright, novelist and short story writer. He is Professor Emeritus in Creative Writing at the University of Aberdeen, where he founded the WORD Festival. With his wife he runs the Sri Chinmoy meditation centre in Edinburgh. His most recent books are the novel *Night Boat*, the poetry collection *Morning Glory* (with Elizabeth Blackadder) and the playscript *No Nothing.*

George Anderson Vetch (1785–1873) went to India in 1807, a lieutenant in the Bengal Native Infantry. After fighting in the Anglo-Nepalese War (1814–16) and being wounded at the siege of Kamaoun, he retired from the army in 1836. Vetch published at least four books of poetry, despite the advice of a reviewer of the first that his military merits were greater than those of his versifying (the reviewer advised that instead of composing poems, Vetch should divert himself by 'fondling his baby, or sit down quietly and take a moderate cup of tea with its nurse'). *Sultry Hours* and *Songs of Exile* (both 1820) were followed by *Dara, or the Minstrel Prince* (1850) and *Milton at Rome* (1851), which he published under the name 'Major Vetch'. *The Gong* (1852) is the story in verse of a Scot's life in India.

Lawrence Augustine Waddell (1854–1938). Born in Greenock, Waddell graduated (1879) with a Master's degree in Chemistry from Glasgow University and became a resident surgeon in Glasgow's Western Infirmary. He joined the Indian Medical Service, accompanying military expeditions with the Bengal Army. In 1881 he was appointed Professor of Chemistry and Pathology, Medical College of Calcutta. He is credited with discovery of Gautama Buddha's lost birthplace at Kapilavastu in the Nepal Terai (stone inscriptions donated to Museum of Calcutta). In 1888 he became Principal Medical Officer for the Darjeeling District and later set out to explore the Himalayas and visited Patna, India. In 1923 he went back to Greenock, moved to the Isle of Bute in 1933 and lived there for the rest of his life. He has been described as the original Indiana Jones. *The British Edda* (1930), is a bizarre epic of conflation: in this work, Adam, Arthur and Thor are one person, Eve and Guinevere are one person, and the Indian deity Kali is also Ymi, Heidi, Ida, El, Kiol or Gulli with her consort Wodan or Bodo. The book attracted the attention of Hugh MacDiarmid in the 1930s and Charles Olson in the 1950s, who said that Waddell 'dances all over this thing, like some damned witch doctor, trying to squeeze out the old and lost history'. The extracts here are from 'Scene I: Vision of Eden & Its Serpent Priestess & Pre-Adamite People' and its oddity speaks for itself.

Rab Wilson (b.1960) Born in New Cumnock, Ayrshire, Wilson served his apprenticeship as an engineer with the National Coal Board and worked in the deep pits until the miners' strike of 1984–85, after which he retrained as a psychiatric nurse. He has been an activist and advocate for the Scots language, a member of the National Committee for the Scots Language Resource Centre, a regular attendee at the parliamentary Cross Party Group for the Scots language at Holyrood and is well-known as a 'whistle-blower' on the injustices of management in the National Health Service, particularly in NHS Ayrshire & Arran. His poems are published in *Accent of the Mind* (2006), *Life Sentence* (2009), *A Map for the Blind* (2011) and *Zero Hours* (2016).

Luath Press Limited

committed to publishing well written books worth reading

LUATH PRESS takes its name from Robert Burns, whose little collie Luath (*Gael.*, swift or nimble) tripped up Jean Armour at a wedding and gave him the chance to speak to the woman who was to be his wife and the abiding love of his life. Burns called one of the 'Twa Dogs' Luath after Cuchullin's hunting dog in Ossian's *Fingal*. Luath Press was established in 1981 in the heart of Burns country, and is now based a few steps up the road from Burns' first lodgings on Edinburgh's Royal Mile. Luath offers you distinctive writing with a hint of unexpected pleasures.

Most bookshops in the UK, the US, Canada, Australia, New Zealand and parts of Europe, either carry our books in stock or can order them for you. To order direct from us, please send a £sterling cheque, postal order, international money order or your credit card details (number, address of cardholder and expiry date) to us at the address below. Please add post and packing as follows: UK – £1.00 per delivery address; overseas surface mail – £2.50 per delivery address; overseas airmail – £3.50 for the first book to each delivery address, plus £1.00 for each additional book by airmail to the same address. If your order is a gift, we will happily enclose your card or message at no extra charge.

Luath Press Limited
543/2 Castlehill
The Royal Mile
Edinburgh EH1 2ND
Scotland
Telephone: +44 (0)131 225 4326 (24 hours)
email: sales@luath. co.uk
Website: www. luath.co.uk